WE CAN'T EVEN
MARCH STRAIGHT

Edmund Hall has written regularly for the *Independent*,
and also for the *Sunday Times*, the London *Evening
Standard* and other newspapers. He has written and pro-
duced for television and radio and his documentary credits
include investigative programmes on drug-smuggling and
mercenaries. He works and lives in London.

In memory of John 'Alex' Mahoney

Edmund Hall

WE CAN'T EVEN
MARCH STRAIGHT

Homosexuality in the British Armed Forces

VINTAGE

Published by Vintage 1995

2 4 6 8 10 9 7 5 3 1

Vintage
Random House
20 Vauxhall Bridge Road, London SW1V 2SA

Random House Australia (Pty) Limited
20 Alfred Street, Milsons Point, Sydney
New South Wales 2061, Australia

Random House New Zealand Limited
18 Poland Road, Glenfield
Auckland 10, New Zealand

Random House South Africa (Pty) Limited
PO Box 337, Bergvlei, South Africa

Random House UK Limited Reg. No. 954009

A CIP catalogue record for this book is available
from the British Library

ISBN 0099495619

Papers used by Random House UK are natural re-
cyclable products made from wood grown in sustainable
forests. The manufacturing processes conform to the
environmental regulations of the country of origin

Typeset in Sabon by SX Composing Ltd, Rayleigh, Essex

Printed and bound in Great Britain by
Cox & Wyman, Reading, Berkshire

A VINTAGE ORIGINAL

Contents

	Acknowledgements	vii
	Introduction: The Same Old Story	1
1	It Happens Every Day	17
2	The Difficult Life of a Woman	34
3	Damage Limitation	50
4	In Support of the Status Quo	67
5	Security Risk	82
6	The Blackmailer's Charter	96
7	Staying in the Closet	112
8	With Rose-Tinted Spectacles?	128
9	Worlds Apart	138
10	Don't Ask – Don't Tell	154
11	The Road to Change	166

ACKNOWLEDGEMENTS

WHEN RANDY SHILTS wrote *Conduct Unbecoming*, about lesbians and gay men in the US Armed Forces in 1989, he brought to the public's attention for the first time the reality of a policy that has caused heart-ache and worse for thousands of men and women across the United States.

I had hoped to meet Randy Shilts when I visited California to research for this book, but unfortunately he died of an AIDS-related illness a few months before I got there. Had I met him, I would have thanked him for putting pen to paper on a subject very close to my own heart. He showed clearly in *Conduct Unbecoming* that there are many lesbians and gay men who can be superb servicemen and women. And people like me, who have lost their jobs as a result of the US and British armed forces' policy on homosexuality, read his book avidly.

Conduct Unbecoming was the opening salvo in a newly invigorated campaign by lesbian and gay groups in the United States to have the ban on them serving in the armed forces dropped. In a comprehensive and detailed analysis, Randy Shilts showed that the ban has no rational basis – it is based on fears about the nature of homosexuality that are demonstrably untrue.

If my book does anything, I hope it will surprise people. I don't believe that many of those who support the ban really know what is done in its name. The Ministry of Defence, when I interviewed them, seemed genuinely surprised by some of the stories I was able to tell them about what has happened to men and women as a result of the policy. The experience of the British armed forces has not been written about before – and we now have the most rigorously enforced exclusionary policy in the Western world.

At the time of writing, a group of men and women are preparing to take the British Government to court over their dismissals. As their cases proceed the mass media will, I'm sure, take a very close interest in their progress, and the debate over the issue will continue. This book covers the issues and arguments that will be a large part of this debate. The men and women challenging their Government in the courts do not want large compensation payments. They simply want the right to serve openly in their own armed forces.

I took up journalism when I lost my job in the Royal Navy in 1988. That I started writing at all is entirely due to Hugh David, who offered me a job as a researcher when I was still wondering what to do with my life. If my intention had been simply to write an angry response to my own dismissal I would have done so then: the book that I have in fact written is the result of a feature I wrote in the *Independent* in August 1993 about an RAF sergeant who lost his job. The response to that feature was overwhelming, and my agent, Peter Robinson at Curtis Brown, pointed out that there was not a British book on the subject and that maybe I should write one. His counsel and advice resulted in a proposal which several publishers were interested in, and his constant enthusiasm and constructive criticism contributed more than anything else to the book's final shape. That we accepted the offer from Random House was due to the fact that my publisher Jonathan Burnham, seemed to have the same vision of the book as I did.

I must thank David Mitchell and Peter Boyce in Perth, Mike Elith and Dale Hardy in Melbourne, Sean Brett and Greg Crockett in Sydney and the staff at the *Sydney Star Observer*, David Browne in Los Angeles, Tom Casesa in New York, and an old friend, Doug Hausman, in Washington DC. I also have to thank a gay-friendly airline, American Airlines, for helping to make my flights less stressful.

ACKNOWLEDGEMENTS

Simon Ingram and David Tolliss put up with my stress in an idyllic cottage in Cheshire, where I wrote most of the book. On my return to London, Rob Hayward let me take over his flat while I finished it.

In no particular order, I also have to mention many other people for their help, support, and encouragement: Angela Mason, Anya Palmer, Suad El-Amin, Roger Goode and Terry Harding at Stonewall; Tracy Charlton at Barclays; *History Today* magazine; Jason Thomas, Edward Montagu, Julian Gibbs, Andrew Cruickshank, Paul Gambaccini, Ian McKellen, Caron Scott, Robert Ely, Mike Sansom, Patrick Lyster-Todd, David Cook, David Prosser, Philip Pollock, Callum Martin, Derek Laud, Stephen Leahy, Jeremy Trafford, Mike O'Halloran, Angus Pope, Ralph Wilde, Will Parry, Adam Morris and all the boys at Adam's Row, Garry Harris, Scott Davidson, Andrew Onraët. To all of them, and to all those I have not named, either at their own request or because of my forgetfulness, my enormous gratitude.

Finally, I must also thank my mother who has been an endless source of support and who even cashed my cheques (sometimes successfully), when my funds ran dry.

Introduction

THE SAME OLD STORY

PEACE, LOVE AND understanding. Meditation and mescalin. The swinging late 1960s were years of emancipation for lesbians and gay men all over the Western world. In Britain in 1967 Parliament was finally persuaded to alter the law under which Oscar Wilde had been imprisoned in the nineteenth century – the 1864 Sexual Offences Act, with its 1885 amendments. This was the law that prohibited sexual acts between men. Then in June 1969 in New York City's Greenwich Village, gay men began three days of rioting in response to yet another raid on the Stonewall gay bar by officers of the New York Police Department. The men barricaded the policemen into the bar, and then attacked the officers who came to rescue their colleagues. These two events saw the birth of a gay political movement on both sides of the Atlantic.

Suddenly lesbian and gay people had a voice. Television documentaries were made about the 'underground homosexual lifestyle' and, although the response was slow at first, in the next twenty-five years life changed beyond recognition for lesbians and gay men in Britain, the United States, Australia, Canada and all over Europe. Formerly clandestine pubs, bars and clubs became the fulcrum of trend and fashion. The pink pound and dollar were big business; and almost every high street newsagent now sells copies of *Gay Times* or the American *Advocate*.

But before these changes, before homosexual activity was legalised between consenting men, before gay men and

1

women in the public eye 'came out', before Martina Navratilova, Boy George, Sir Ian McKellen and the Communards, before *My Own Private Idaho* and Tom Hanks's *Philadelphia*, before AIDS activism, and certainly before mainstream advertisers and publishers caught on to the economic power that homosexuals keep in their wallets, life was very different. Many lesbians and gay men lived a fairly terrifying life on the fringes of society. A known homosexual could expect regular visits from the police; and if caught committing an 'unnatural' act he could expect to go to prison; or at the very least to be lectured by a magistrate on the dangers of a deviant lifestyle. The police examined a homosexual's address book and diary in minute detail: in Britain it was common for official promises of immunity from prosecution to be given in return for a list of other 'named' homosexuals. Young, 'pretty' policemen were used as bait to trap the unwary homosexual into a charge of 'importuning'. Fortunately most of these practices have now been rightly consigned to the history books. At least, they have been for the civilian.

There is one section of the community for whom nothing has changed at all since the pre-1967 days of witch-hunts and secrecy.

Lesbian and gay men and women serving in Britain's armed forces continue to live with the constant fear of blackmail, exposure, loss of career, ruin by informants or spies, the threat of repeated investigation and interrogation, sometimes stripsearches and forced physical examinations, even warrantless raids on their homes. Their lives are more like those of the pre-decriminalisation world, the world of secrecy and personal tragedy which affected people like Lord Montagu of Beaulieu, Joe Orton and Kenneth Williams. Members of the armed forces enjoy none of the modern privileges or rights of their civilian colleagues if they happen to be lesbian or gay.

The Government, through the Ministry of Defence, states that homosexuality is incompatible with military life, and that any member of the armed forces who is found to be homosexual, or who admits to being homosexual, will be discharged. According to the Ministry, there are no circumstances in which a lesbian or gay man would be allowed to serve openly in any of the services.

The current policy, issued in 1994, says:

> Homosexuality, whether male or female, is considered incompatible with service in the Armed Forces. This is not only because of the close physical conditions in which personnel often have to live and work, but also because homosexual behaviour can cause offence, polarise relationships, induce ill-discipline, and as a consequence damage morale and unit effectiveness. If individuals admit to being homosexual whilst serving and their Commanding Officer judges that this admission is well-founded they will be required to leave the Services. The Armed Forces policy was supported by the Select Committee on the Armed Forces Bill 1991, who stated in their report that they were not persuaded that the time had come to require the Armed Forces to accept homosexuals or homosexual activity. However, the committee recommended, and the MOD accepted, that homosexual activity of a kind that is legal in civilian law should not constitute an offence under Service Law.

In pursuing this policy, the armed forces discharged 260 men and women between 1991 and 1994 specifically for homosexuality. It seems likely that a substantially larger number resigned in cases where the issue of sexuality was a major factor. Many individuals, for example, are given the chance to resign rather than be discharged involuntarily if they are found to be homosexual. A large number of men and women choose to leave the services for personal reasons connected with their sexuality, but manage to do so without the Ministry of Defence ever knowing that they were lesbian or gay. Of the lesbian and gay people interviewed for this book, well under half had been specifically discharged for being gay. These proportions are also reflected by the membership of Rank Outsiders, a support group for men and women affected by the current policy. A truer figure for the number of individuals lost to the armed forces between 1990 and 1994 is therefore probably around 600.

The Ministry of Defence will not release any figures for the years before 1990, claiming that they have never been compiled, and that it would involve disproportionate cost to do so. But the level of discharges for homosexuality is probably no higher now than it has been in the past. During the 1970s and 1980s there was a series of 'witch-hunts', in which detailed investigations and interviews with a few lesbians or gay men led on to more and more names, until the trail ran cold, and all involved could be dismissed. Cyprus, Hong Kong, and individual Royal Navy warships all had their own witch-hunts during these years. These witch-hunts still happen, although individuals are less likely to hand over names of lesbian and gay colleagues now. During the 1970s and early 1980s there was still a very real chance of spending time in prison for committing an offence that was legal in civilian life. But before the 1970s prison was far more common, as it was in civilian life.

Britain is now effectively alone in NATO in maintaining an exclusionary rule which is actively enforced. The United States, after a very public argument between Clinton's White House and the Pentagon, backpedalled from a campaign promise to lift the ban completely, and instead created the so-called 'Don't ask – Don't tell' compromise. The Clinton Administration maintains that this policy is a step forward for lesbians and gay men who are members of the two million strong US military machine. But American lesbian and gay lobby groups believe that in reality the new policy is no different to the old, and there are at present around 130 cases before various federal courts attempting to challenge the present policy. The 'Don't ask – Don't tell' rule means that in theory no investigative officer in the US armed forces can ask about someone's sexuality, and no individual within the armed forces is required to give information about their sexual life. However, in the event of a member of the US forces being discovered to be lesbian or gay, he or she will still be automatically discharged. After a year in operation it looks as though the new policy will result in the loss of at least 600 jobs annually. Between 1980 and 1990, 16,919 gay US servicemen and women lost their jobs, which works out at about 1,500 a year, so the numbers seem to have reduced somewhat since the Clinton Administration's policy took effect.

Currently Britain is a long way from the US model. The British armed forces continue to ask servicemen and women if they are lesbian and gay, and each service has its own police force investigating homosexuality: the Royal Military Police (RMP) and Special Investigating Branch, the RAF Police and Security Services (P&SS), the Royal Navy's Regulating Branch and Special Investigating Branch (SIB). These three departments actively seek out servicemen and women they suspect of homosexuality. Detailed and expensive investigations are instigated in order to uncover possible homosexuals, often involving lengthy 'undercover' surveillance. It is not even necessary for the investigators to prove that homosexual conduct has taken place, the fact that an individual is 'intrinsically' homosexual is sufficient to lead to his or her automatic dismissal.

In some ways the liberalisation of British society's understanding of homosexuality has damaged the position of serving gays. Before 1967 the policies used by the armed forces were specifically aimed at outlawing homosexual behaviour: there seems to have been no comprehension in the military establishment of an individual's intrinsic sexuality. The modern world generally accepts now that some people are homosexual and that it is their nature to be attracted to members of their own sex, but this is a relatively new understanding of the 'condition'. Until homosexual emancipation, sexual activity between members of the same sex was more often viewed simply as deviant, a condition requiring a cure, or a criminal act. This meant that a non-practising lesbian or gay man would not risk dismissal. The situation in the armed forces now is more enlightened as to the nature of homosexuality, but at the same time less forgiving to the non-practising homosexual.

The 1994 policy deals with this situation in terms of potential new recruits: if a potential recruit admits to being homosexual, but states that he/she does not at present nor in the future intend to engage in homosexual activity, he/she will not be enlisted.

John Beck was discharged from the RAF in 1992 for being

a non-practising homosexual. He admitted that he had homosexual feelings, but as a religious man did not wish to act on them. His bosses at the Ministry of Defence did not find this situation acceptable and he lost his job. He now wishes to become a priest, and the Church seems to accept that he can be both gay and chaste. It seems that even the Church is more liberal than the Ministry of Defence in this regard.

In financial terms alone, the cost of the current policy is substantial. In the last two years at least four pilots have left the Royal Air Force and the Fleet Air Arm after it was discovered that they were homosexual. They include, for example, a helicopter warfare instructor and a maritime reconnaissance pilot who, taken together, had over twenty years of service. The cost of training these two individuals over the years will have easily exceeded £3 million. A senior lieutenant-commander in the Royal Navy left the service because his lover was dying, and he felt unable to care for his partner and conceal his private life at work. His departure will cost the MOD another £0.5 million or so.

The Ministry does not publicly calculate the cost of its policy of excluding lesbians and gay men from serving, which makes it very difficult to estimate accurately the policy's true cost. The US General Accounting Office (GAO) encountered similar problems in 1992 when it tried to calculate the cost to the US military of its similar exclusionary policy. The only figures that the GAO were able to find were the costs of initial basic training of enlisted men and officers, and for 1990 these were estimated at $28,226 (£18,818) for each enlisted man, and $120,772 (£80,515) for each officer. The British policy clearly costs tens of millions of pounds on an annual basis if all training, experience lost to the service, and investigations are added together. In Britain we need the same level of training facilities that the American forces use, but we train fewer people. The cost of maintaining these facilities is therefore spread out over a smaller number of men and women. If, conservatively, we suggest basic training, salary and administration costs of £100,000 for each officer, and £30,000 for each enlisted man or woman, and that their trade training, advanced training and gaining of experience costs about the same again, we can try to roughly estimate the cost. Allowing for a ratio of other ranks to officers of twelve to one the current policy has cost between £40 million and £50 million since 1990.

Fifty million pounds, in MOD speak, 'buys a lot of kit'. A useful force of light armoured vehicles from Vickers in Newcastle for example, or the complete internal and external communications (satellite, VHF, UHF and so on) system for two new amphibious assault ships to replace HMS *Fearless* and *Intrepid*, and there would still be £7 million or so left in small change. At an average salary of £25,000 a year, lifting the ban could pay for an additional 600 or so members of the armed forces – nearly a whole battalion of infantry, or the complete complement of three Royal Navy frigates.

The current ban is not expensive only in financial terms, the emotional cost to those affected is substantial too.

RAF Sergeant Simon Ingram is a successful young man, twice recommended for commission as an officer and the proud holder of a Gulf Medal for service during the liberation of Kuwait in 1991. Sergeant Ingram is also a homosexual. He tried to keep his sexuality quiet, since he was well aware that honesty would result in immediate dismissal and that he could face a court martial. However, Simon made a mistake; he trusted a few close friends and colleagues with the truth about his personal life. One of these colleagues used his knowledge of Simon's homosexuality as a bargaining chip with the RAF Police when he himself was in trouble of his own, and the military machine for dealing with 'homosexuality and other unnatural behaviour' swung into action.

And so, like many others on different days throughout the year, on Tuesday 26 January 1993 Sergeant Ingram sat for the last time with the rest of his Nimrod crew in the flight briefing room at RAF Kinloss in Scotland. He was preparing to fly out over the sea looking for submarines on a routine training mission. The Nimrod's captain, a flight-lieutenant, was going through the final briefing details, but while Simon tried to pay attention he was increasingly conscious of nervous tension building up inside him. His fifteen colleagues on the Nimrod crew sat listening to the details of the operation they were to take part in, but his mind was elsewhere.

Before the briefing Simon had seen the senior squadron leader speak to his flight-lieutenant and he sensed that he was in trouble. As the briefing finished and the aircrew began to leave the room and go to their aircraft Simon was stopped by the squadron leader: 'Simon, you won't be going flying.'

One of Simon's crew asked him if everything was OK, and Simon shook his head. 'I think my air force career is about to come to an end,' he remembers saying.

Lesbians and gay men in the armed forces are always waiting to be caught. The feeling that gripped Simon – the breathless, nauseous, premonitory panic – is always only a few seconds away. Serving lesbians and gays know that surveillance is regularly carried out by the armed forces' own police forces on gay and lesbian clubs and pubs. Several people have compared the intensity of feeling that hits you when you know you've been caught to a powerful drug rush.

Simon and his squadron leader walked over to the RAF police building and went into a small grey interview room. He was met there by two members of the RAF's investigation unit (P&SS), and after tapes had been inserted into the recording machine and all present had identified themselves, the investigating officer said what Simon had feared most:

'We are here to investigate you for alleged homosexual tendencies.'

All the men and women I have spoken to while preparing this book remember the moment when they were first told that the 'system' was on to them with unambiguous clarity. They have talked about anger and shock, sometimes relief, often panic. The moment of realisation can take the form of enormous relief that years of worry and secrecy have come to an end; but more often the feeling is bitter as the realisation comes that years of careful covering up have been in vain.

As the interview progresses the guilty 'suspect' comes to realise that his or her life is going to change immeasurably in the weeks and months that follow.

8

The attempts to investigate and prove homosexuality are not casual – the results of complaints by colleagues, for example – but pro-active detailed investigations involving the whole range of surveillance skills open to the various investigative branches of the armed forces.

In early 1994 two RAF officers suspected of homosexuality were placed under surveillance for about four weeks. It is impossible to discover for certain how extensive the operation was, although the two officers have been led to believe that ten men were used to follow them. The MOD will not discuss operational matters of this nature or the cost involved, but the operation resulted in a report to the officers' commanding officer which stated that, after receiving an anonymous letter which made allegations that two RAF officers were gay, an investigation had been carried out and evidence collected which supported the allegations. The two individuals, both of whom received extremely expensive flight training, are awaiting confirmation of their dismissal at the time of writing.

Another young man in one of the so-called élite regiments of the British army spent most of the summer of 1994 wondering how to break it to his parents that the trouble he had been getting into for the last six months had been caused not by 'an attitude problem', as his commanding officer had called it, but by him coming to terms with the fact that he is gay and not knowing what to do about it. Should he 'out' himself and get thrown out? Should he deny his sexual feelings, get married and try to pretend? Or should he plan to lead a double life, inventing torrid nights with girlfriends for the sake of his colleagues, while in reality using saunas, sleazy bars and public toilets to fulfil his sexual desires?

There is another option for those who believe the net is closing in on them – suicide. The combination of imminent loss of career and home, and the need to explain why to a wife, child or parent – added to the trauma of trying to come to terms with the fact that one is homosexual – can be too much for some.

There are a number of suicides in the armed forces, most often among junior members. The Ministry of Defence says this is tragic but inevitable in an environment which is by its nature highly stressful. It is not always possible to know the complexities of the reasons why a young man or woman has taken such drastic action, and problems with their sexuality may only partly explain why they have decided to take their own life.

There is anecdotal evidence from several of the men and women interviewed for this book that sexuality has been a factor in several cases of suicide over the years. However, since in none of those cases has the suggestion been made public, it would be invidious to cite them. If those who took their own lives left notes saying that they were doing so because they were lesbian or gay, then those notes have never been released by the MOD. Perhaps the experience of a 24-year-old man who was discharged from the army in 1994 demonstrates how close thoughts of suicide are for many:

'I got home and sat down wondering what to do. I lived alone and had to call and tell someone what had happened. What was I supposed to say? Hello Mum, I'm being thrown out of the army and I'm a poof? I sat there for hours while it got dark wondering what to do. I lost hours and hours just staring at the wall, deciding that it would be easier if I killed myself. I thought about all the ways of doing it, remember looking in the drawer at the pills and trying to work out how many I would need. In the end the phone rang and it was my mum. I was crying on the phone and she didn't know why. I couldn't tell her what the problem was. In the end she drove down about four hours to come and see me, and then I told her.'

In another case an RAF NCO in intelligence was investigated at length in Germany — he didn't name any other gay servicemen, but a colleague at work killed himself unexpectedly three weeks after the investigations began. The former NCO believes that the pressure of waiting for the 'witch-hunt' trail to lead to him was more than he could bear.

The debate about whether or not lesbians and gay men can and should be able to serve in Britain's armed forces continues to take its place high up on the media's 'sexy stories' agenda. As a group of sacked men and women are currently taking the British Government to the European Court, it seems likely that this issue will continue to hog the headlines on a regular basis.

The increasingly vocal and experienced gay political lobby, in the form of groups like Stonewall and Outrage, is ensuring that in Britain, in much the same way as in the United States, the mainstream governmental and legislative ear cannot fail to hear the lesbian and gay voice. Opponents of homosexual law reform talk about the insidious advance of the 'homo-sexualist propagandist', but for the most part the continued pressure by groups like these has resulted in campaign promises from political parties on the left, and a new pre-paredness to listen by those on the right.

Until now the arguments for and against change have only been aired in the charged atmosphere of political debate or television chat shows and news bulletins. It is time for an ana-lysis of the arguments for and against change to see whether there really is a compelling case on either side. This book looks at those affected by the current policy – and examines the situation in countries which manage to defend themselves without excluding lesbians and gay men from their armed forces.

I have to declare my interest in the proceedings from the outset. I was sacked from the Royal Navy in 1988 when I admitted, after a great deal of stress and soul-searching, that I was gay. I do not believe that my sexuality presented any sort of threat to my colleagues, or jeopardised my ability to do my job effectively and well. I chose to 'come out', and so had time to prepare myself for the ensuing interrogation and dismissal; but most of the 260 men and women discharged specifically for homosexuality since 1990 did not have that choice – they were caught, found out, trapped as the result of surveillance or informants, or felt forced to make an admission as investigations began to get too close for comfort.

The position of the lesbians and gays who are not caught is also examined – because, as the MOD acknowledges, those who are caught and sacked because of their sexuality must

11

represent only a proportion of the total number of lesbians and gays serving. Many of those who do continue to serve, and those who have served and retired, suggest that their distinguished records alone prove that lesbians and gay men can serve satisfactorily.

Throughout NATO, and other armed forces around the world, lesbians and gays serve openly and with distinction. At the time of writing, 'out' gay Dutch soldiers were serving in Bosnia and Rwanda – while in Australia, Canada and New Zealand it is now an offence to discriminate against lesbian and gay servicemen and women. What is it about the social climate in Britain that requires us to spend money enforcing a policy other countries no longer feel they need?

John Wilkinson, a Conservative Member of Parliament, and Chairman of the Special House of Commons Select Committee on the Armed Forces in 1991, said in response to these points: 'How we run our armed forces is a matter for the British Parliament and people alone. It is the view of the forces, and has been the view of successive Governments that it would be inappropriate to insist that the forces accept these people. People's sexuality runs very deep and it affects the way in which people get on with their colleagues. It can prejudice their behaviour in an invidious way.'

It was this committee which recommended the change in the armed forces' regulations on homosexuality that has been widely described as 'decriminalisation'. Before these changes homosexuality was a criminal offence in the armed forces – meaning that it could be tried by court martial and was potentially punishable by a prison sentence. 'Decriminalisation' means that acts which are legal in civilian life will no longer be treated as criminal in service life. The MOD accepted these changes, and the legislation to enact them was included in the Criminal Justice Act of 1994.

However, the 'decriminalisation' in reality has not changed life for those men and women affected by it, as the complete ban on service by lesbians and gay men remains in place. The fact that being gay is no longer a criminal offence does not mean that the investigations are carried out any less vigorously than before. The 1994 guidelines also make very clear that the armed forces retain the right to take action against offenders on the basis that their activities are 'contrary to good service order and discipline', for example.

When it is so abundantly clear that the armed forces don't want to employ lesbians and gays in the first place, why on earth do so many want to join? Quite simply because a large number of the men and women who have been thrown out did not realise that they were gay when they joined. Retrospectively it's easy for most gay people to say that they knew they were homosexual from a very early age – but it can take a long time for an individual man or woman to acknowledge their homosexuality, even to themselves. In the style of speech learnt from their therapists, Americans talk about 'denial', the period of our lives during which our conscious mind refuses to accept the reality about ourselves that, deep down, we probably know. Those men and women who have joined the armed forces knowing that they are gay and intending to lead a double life are fewer and tend to be older, university graduates, for example. Those who have joined knowing they were gay have asked why their sexuality should prevent them from having the right to defend their country. Unfortunately these men and women are not able to ask this question publicly – to do so would result in immediate dismissal.

A number of supporters of the ban, including Walter Sweeney, a Conservative MP, have said that since everyone knows that the ban is in place, it is the individual's own fault if he or she is found out and has to be sacked. We have already seen that there are many who are unaware of their homosexuality when they join – at fifteen, sixteen, seventeen years of age – but those who consciously lie about their sexuality argue that they are right to do so.

In the First World War, boys who lied about their age in order to join the army and defend their country were young heroes; men and women who join now and lie about their sexuality in order to defend their country are seen as liars and cheats. Lying about your eyesight, your height, your hearing, your fitness, your age, your qualifications – all these are traditional and somehow respected, as they only go to show how patriotic and determined an individual is. To lie about being gay though – to supporters of the ban that is entirely different.

When I joined the navy directly after leaving school I had no idea that I was gay. I had had a few sexual experiences with other boys at public school, but I also had girlfriends and assumed that after joining the navy I would carry on going out with women, and that eventually I would get married and have children. Within eighteen months, through friends from school who were at university in London, I had met a number of gay people and found that I identified with them. It was not an immediate process – I visited my first gay bar whilst in the navy and spent about five minutes there before leaving in a state of panic. But I went back twenty-four hours later. I discovered more about myself, gradually, over a period of months.

My experience was not unusual, and so when the MOD look at the list of discharges since 1990 they should be aware that this issue is of great importance not just to those who have been dismissed, but also to those who remain in the services, carrying out their jobs on a regular day-to-day basis. For the squadron leader who was discharged in 1991 there must be other gay men of the same rank still serving; for the four majors and four captains who have been sacked from the army in the last four years there must be others still turning up for duty whilst remaining 'in the closet'; and for the 113 privates and 35 able seamen who have lost their jobs since 1990 there must be hundreds still serving.

If all these individuals were uncovered at once the MOD would have a large number of discharges to handle. It would also make clear the large role lesbians and gay men actually play in the armed forces. I spoke to a journalist who researched the position and status of women in the armed forces after the Gulf War, who said she was staggered to find how many of the women she spoke to were almost openly lesbian.

There are interviews in this book with men and women who are still serving, who intend to continue serving, and who are also lesbian or gay – they have spoken to me on the basis of my guarantee of complete confidentiality. Wherever I have agreed to treat somebody's contribution as confidential I have had to change substantial details about their service and background in order to ensure that the investigative branches of the service police forces will not be able to use this book as a series of clues. I do not want to be accused of starting a witch-hunt of my own.

In these cases, instead of leaving great chunks blank I have replaced the sensitive details with others, agreed with the interviewee, which give the same impression as the facts, but which will confuse anyone who tries to identify them. In some cases I have changed the service completely because the real career pattern is too individual. For these deliberate inaccuracies I apologise. Perhaps before too long the policy will change and it will be time for another book, in which serving lesbians and gays are able to talk openly – but for now this is as close as we are going to get.

I

IT HAPPENS EVERY DAY

'WE NEED TO have a few words with you.'

'I don't think you'll be going flying.'

'We are separating you from the rest of the ship's company for your own safety.'

'You are being flown to Portsmouth for questioning.'

There's nothing subtle about the arrival of the service police once they believe they have the evidence to prove that an individual man or woman is homosexual. As soon as is possible after the evidence has been received the individual concerned is separated from his or her place of work and questioned at length.

RAF Corporal Ian Waterhouse was discharged from the RAF in 1994. Ian, from the north-west of England, has hung on to his northern accent even after twelve years of service life, and has little of the snappy brevity of speech often associated with serving NCOs. He had spent the last six years of his time in the RAF as an active gay man serving at bases in Belgium and Germany. After all that time Ian felt pretty secure in his job as an administrative clerk at RAF Uxbridge. But in the autumn of 1993 the RAF police swooped. The confidential official documents outlining what happened in his case are worth quoting at some length as they demonstrate the current process of investigation and confrontation very well.

On 13 September 1993 [a former serviceman] alleged that Waterhouse was homosexual. [. . .] was interviewed and he

17

stated that during July 1992 he saw Waterhouse in the company of an unidentified male companion at the 'Europride Gay March' which took place in London. He stated that they had spoken briefly and he opined that Waterhouse appeared shocked at having been seen. [. . .] said that he believed Waterhouse to be homosexual, but that he could offer no evidence to substantiate his beliefs. He declined the opportunity to make a statement.

At RAF Uxbridge on 16 September 1993, Waterhouse was interviewed after caution. He admitted he was homosexual. He consented to a search of his Service accommodation. However, the items impounded were subsequently deemed to be of no evidential value and were later returned to him.

A re-interview took place at RAF Uxbridge on 27 September 1993. He admitted to having had homosexual relations with no more than four civilians since joining the RAF in 1982. The relationships varied in duration. He stated that the first time he had a homosexual affair was when he was serving at SHAPE (Supreme Headquarters Allied Powers Europe) in Belgium from March 1988 until January 1990. The man concerned was a civilian. Corporal Waterhouse gave no evidence to establish that any of the homosexual acts to which he has admitted have taken place in public or have involved a partner under the age of twenty-one years.

There is no evidence to suggest that Corporal Waterhouse is, or has been involved in homosexual relationships with any member of HM Forces, or that criminal offences have been committed during the course of those relationships. Waterhouse has confessed that he is a homosexual, although there is no evidence to suggest misconduct, corruption, blatant or promiscuous activities or unnatural behaviour on Service establishments. Waterhouse was offered medical advice in accordance with RAF GAI 7008, an offer he subsequently declined.

There was a seven-month delay while Ian Waterhouse waited to be told officially that he was being sacked and to be given a date for his last day of service. Although he was being sacked, he was required to continue working throughout this period. The inconsistency of a policy which requires Corporal Waterhouse to be sacked because of his sexuality and yet requires him to continue to work out his notice is clear. If his sexuality presents such a problem in the workplace that he needs to be dismissed, why is he still able to carry out his normal duties?

These duties included regular spells as an armed guard at the gates of RAF Uxbridge. For some months after the investigation, knowing that he was going to be sacked, Waterhouse, whom one could expect to be suffering from depression and who was undoubtedly angry with his employers, was spending long periods of time alone with his rifle in west London.

'I was given an SA80 automatic rifle and live ammunition and went on duty at the gate. You have to retake a test regularly before you are allowed to do guard with live weapons, and I retook and had my green card stamped on 30 October and 30 November 1993. I was feeling down about things of course, and if they had really got to me, I suppose, if I had been really screwed up by everything I could have fired it at the dual-carriageway by the gate or at the woman who lived in the house opposite.'

In a statement to his superiors at the time he said: 'It seems so stupid that since 16 September 1993 I have been allowed to work in a normal environment for six months afterwards, if six months, why not six years, a question that no one seems to have an answer for.'

In theory at least, the procedures for discharge from the armed forces should be pretty much the same, irrespective of the circumstances of the case or which service the man or woman happens to be a member of. Since the publication of Joint Service Guidelines on Homosexuality in 1994, commanding officers and security departments in the navy, army, and RAF are using the same information when making decisions about possible homosexuals in their units.

All suspected homosexuals are interviewed, by service police if possible, but by their commanding officer or head of department if not. The interview which is conducted by the service police includes a number of automatic areas of questioning.

First the interviewer will want to satisfy himself that the accused (this is after all an interview under caution, now taped, and carried out in accordance with the Police and Criminal Evidence Act [PACE] 1984), is genuinely homosexual. RAF Sergeant Simon Ingram, dismissed in August 1993 after a colleague reported that Simon had told him he was gay, was asked, ' . . . have you ever kissed a man?'

Brett Burnell, discharged from the Royal Navy for homosexuality in December 1993 had been under surveillance for some time and had been photographed leaving Drummonds, a known gay pub in Portsmouth. He was asked about his visits there. It appears that the navy's SIB use the Department of Social Security offices opposite the pub to carry out surveillance from time to time.

Sam Waters, an army cook from Aldershot, was asked if he liked 'to be active or passive' by a Royal Military Police investigator during his questioning in 1991. An up-front blatant question seems to be the standard opening in these situations. Perhaps the intention is to shock the 'accused' into an immediate admission. If so, it seems to be a fairly ineffective technique, since a large proportion of those interviewed under these circumstances strenuously deny the allegations at first. Simon Ingram refused to answer the questions and listened as the investigating officer started to read out parts of a statement that made detailed allegations about his personal life. Brett Burnell told the investigator that they must have made a mistake. The army cook, in the same tone as the interviewer, asserted his masculinity, and told him to 'fuck off'.

Simon Ingram, speaking about six months after the interview, said: 'What surprised me was the intensity of the questions, they really thought that they could get me to talk just by asking lots of difficult questions. I guess it worked though, because when they mentioned my boyfriend David, who is a civilian, I told them angrily to leave him out of it. You're under a lot of pressure and you make mistakes.'

The investigating officer asked if it was true that Simon Ingram had had a gay man visit his house.

'I was staggered and numb. Trying to remember the details of it all is hard. I know that I tried to deny it for a while, but when they asked about my boyfriend, who is a civilian doctor, I probably protested too much – I was so angry that they had brought David into it. I said that I thought I had better speak to a lawyer, and they took me to a room with a telephone and gave me a list of solicitors. I sat in that room for at least forty minutes doing nothing, just staring at the wall. Eventually I phoned home and found that David had gone out. My lodger was home, and I asked him to phone Stonewall and Rank Outsiders in London to ask for advice. They said I should not say anything until I had got more advice, and that I should call a solicitor. I picked a name from the list I had been given and phoned. I have subsequently been told that the solicitor I spoke to is an honorary member of the Officers' Mess, but he seemed helpful.'

Brett's story is not very different. He remembers being given the impression that the investigators knew everything about him and that it would be futile to lie. The sense of honour and honesty that had been drummed into all young members of the armed forces began to work on their consciences – despite the fact that they both felt strongly that they had a moral right to lie. Both Brett and Simon recall feeling guilty about refusing to admit their homosexuality. They were clear in their own minds that the investigations themselves were morally wrong, but they felt that the onus was on them to tell the truth.

Brett Burnell was interviewed in Portsmouth on the day that his ship, the frigate HMS *Active*, was leaving for Plymouth, and so he missed its sailing. It is difficult to imagine a more significant event for a sailor than to miss the sailing of his ship. Brett Burnell denied all the allegations made by the SIB investigators, and they decided to allow him to rejoin the ship while the investigation continued. He had to travel to Plymouth by train to meet HMS *Active*, and when he got back on board faced intensive questioning from colleagues about the reason for his absence. Fortunately, the navy's bush telegraph had not yet caught up with the reason for his delay, and he was able to rejoin his Mess without serious problems.

But as the next night and day wore on, Brett Burnell became more and more worried about what 'they' might know.

He knew that any detailed investigation would turn up the truth, and he was not prepared to risk it. Although he was relatively new to the Portsmouth gay scene, he had become too well known to people in the pubs and clubs of Plymouth to expect any serious investigation to fail to 'prove' his homosexuality.

After thinking the possibilities over, and finding that he couldn't cope with the constant fear that he was just about to be caught, Brett telephoned the senior investigator at HMS *Nelson* in Portsmouth and told him that he had more to say. The investigators came straight down the next morning and interviewed him again.

'I wasn't telling you the truth yesterday,' said Brett, 'I am gay.'

Simon Ingram was allowed home after his first interview in the knowledge that the investigation into his sex life was going to continue. His boss 'suggested' that he take a couple of days' leave. When his boyfriend, David, arrived home that afternoon he found Simon sitting upset in the living room, and asked why he wasn't flying. Simon replied that he didn't think he would be flying any more.

Simon and David both knew that the RAF police have been known to search servicemen's homes for evidence of homosexuality. They went through their house that evening removing anything that could suggest that they were gay and hiding it in David's car. Possession of the *Pink Paper* or *Gay Times*, or even a 'safer sex' leaflet aimed at gay men could be enough to incriminate Simon. A packet of stronger than average condoms marketed to gay men could signal the end of his career, as could a tube of KY jelly. The atmosphere of paranoia that surrounds any items which could associate a gay serviceman with a homosexual lifestyle is hardly conducive to 'safer sex'.

Ian Waterhouse had his accommodation searched, in spite of his straightforward admission that he was gay. Two RAF policemen took him back to his room and searched all his possessions thoroughly. He recalls the episode: 'When they came to search my room, I found the situation very distressing, I had just been questioned and had a terrible headache and felt sick. An RAF corporal in uniform searched my room and I watched as they pulled everything out of my cupboards and drawers. I have always kept all my things very organised – like you're supposed to in the military, and I felt as if I was being burgled as I watched my stuff being pulled out and dropped all over the place. They took my address book and any piece of paper with a phone number on it. They took a couple of gay story books as well and all of the videos I had that weren't labelled. I presumed that they were looking for items that proved I was gay, but if that was the case they acted pretty weirdly because when they came to my videos of *Torch Song Trilogy* and *Another Country* they left them there – I told them that these were gay classics, but they didn't touch them. They were just looking for material to try and find if I had committed some other offence.'

Like Brett, Simon realised soon that he couldn't deny the allegations indefinitely; he was living with his boyfriend, and had no intention of ending that relationship. Both Simon and Brett say that they had reached a stage when they were determined to tell the truth, and tell it loudly, because they did not believe they had done anything wrong. Two days after his original interview with the RAF police, Simon put on his uniform and went back to his squadron building. As he walked through the door, he was stopped by an older sergeant who was well known and well liked. The sergeant took Simon's hand and said, 'I think what you're doing is incredible.' With the sergeant's good-luck wishes boosting Simon's morale considerably, Simon walked into the squadron leader's office and told him that he was gay. Simon recalls: 'The squadron leader took me to see his boss, the wing commander, and I told him too that I was gay. They were both extremely sensitive and sympathetic, and the wing commander asked what I wanted to happen now. I told him that I just wanted to be left alone to do my job.'

Ian Waterhouse in his response to the allegations, wrote: 'I must state that all I wish is to be left alone to do the job which it seems has been excellently carried out for the past twelve years.'

At twenty-six, Sergeant Simon Ingram was a successful electronics operator who was looking forward to becoming responsible for monitoring and testing the performance of the other air electronics operators in his branch. He did not want to leave the RAF, and apart from his sexuality, there was no reason why he should.

Corporal Ian Waterhouse was an experienced administrative clerk who was used to dealing with personnel matters and had completed four postings in the United Kingdom and two overseas. He had been re-engaged by the RAF on his promotion to corporal in 1988 and was under contract to be employed until 2004 – the RAF would not promote and re-engage an individual for a twenty-two-year contract if it was less than happy with their conduct and ability.

Brett Burnell was an able seaman and a qualified sonar operator who had passed all his technical exams and had no record of any disciplinary problems. Although at the beginning of his career, he had every reason, looking at his record, to expect to have the opportunity to continue it.

Women experience the same process of investigation and discharge. Lieutenant Elaine Chambers was a nursing officer with Queen Alexandra's Royal Army Nursing Corps with an unblemished disciplinary record over nearly six years. She had completed a wide range of highly technical exams, was responsible for a number of junior nurses and was regularly in charge of the whole British military hospital in Hanover at night. She was sacked in 1988 after allegations were made that she had 'made passes' at other women. The allegations, made by another lesbian trying to demonstrate that she was not gay, were later withdrawn. But as a result of the investigation it was discovered that she had had relationships with women, and so she was discharged. The investigation into Elaine's diaries and letters went right round the world, and five women were sacked, in Britain, in Germany and in Hong Kong. Between them they had more than fifty years of service. This was an example of one of the periodic witch-hunts that the armed forces initiate when they find that one name or interview leads them on to another.

All these men and women lost their jobs after being involuntarily 'outed' in one way or another. Their interviews and discharges followed the same pattern. They began with intensely personal questions during a formal police interview under caution, followed by hints of further misconduct to be uncovered, and culminated in automatic dismissal.

These interviews take place in a police interrogation room – not dissimilar to a civilian police questioning room. It has wooden table and chairs – and a tape-recording machine that records simultaneously on to two cassettes. One will be sealed into a plastic evidence bag at the end of the interview, and the other will be used to make a transcription, the working copy. The suspect is issued with a 'Notice to Suspects' which outlines his or her rights – and the questioning begins.

Simon, Elaine, and Brett all had the right to have a solicitor or a service colleague present during the interviews. But because of the embarrassing nature of the situation, most men and women do not take up this option immediately. So they approach this first, crucial interview without the benefit of legal advice or moral support. The questions are not couched in general terms, but are startlingly specific – someone has taught the service police the fine detail of what lesbians and gay men do in bed.

'What did you do in bed with him?'

'So which fingers did she use on you?'

'Is that how you normally have sex with him?'

'Was there anything strange about the way he acted in bed?'

'Was he violent at all?'

Not all men and women under investigation feel that they need to answer all these questions. One cold Tuesday morning at the beginning of February 1993, Simon Ingram, the bright young RAF sergeant with experience of active service in the Gulf War, was called back for a further interview with the investigating officer from the RAF police.

'Sergeant Ingram, I believe you made a statement to your commanding officer. Could you repeat that for the record?'

Simon confirmed that he was gay, but found that his admission was not sufficient. The investigating officer asked him,

25

'Do you have sex with other men?' Simon agreed that since he was gay this seemed likely and that yes he did indeed have sex with other men, although not perhaps as indiscriminately as the question implied.

The investigating officer asked Simon if he was having a relationship with David – Simon replied that as far as he was concerned that had nothing to do with the RAF. After it became clear that Simon was not going to answer any more questions, the investigating officer gave up and finished the interview. While the tape was still running, however, the officer said to Simon,

'If you want to know, my personal feelings on the matter are that it's stupid.'

This experience of support and understanding, from investigators as well as colleagues, is surprisingly common. Perhaps these members of the services' police forces have a greater knowledge of the realities of homosexual life than those whose experience is based on barrack-room gossip and speculation. The commander who formally told Brett that he was to be discharged from the Royal Navy spoke to him privately before the formal proceedings. He told Brett that his personal views differed strongly from the official line, but that this was not a discretionary issue. As the Joint Service Guidelines make clear, 'They will be required to leave the Services'.

Almost all the men and women in this book who have lost their jobs have been surprised by the level of support they have subsequently received from former colleagues. They have had letters and phone calls from their units saying how sorry people are to see them go. Many have leaving parties, get given tankards or sets of crystal glasses.

Rather surprisingly, after an admission of homosexuality has been made, it is part of the responsibility of the investigative branches to determine whether or not it is a genuine admission. Perhaps they are worried that a lot of heterosexual men and women will publicly announce their homosexuality in order to get sacked and be given an engraved tankard by their colleagues.

In order to 'prove' that the admission is genuine, the investigator will ask the 'suspect' very detailed questions about physical sexual practices.

'Do you know what I mean by active and passive?' is a common question. Sam, the army cook, was asked this and further questions: 'Do you kiss him, properly?' for example.

Once the service police have finished going through address books, lockers and other personal belongings, they will try to ascertain what they can from the objects that they find: 'There seem to be mostly men in your address book,' Brett Burnell was told. 'Don't you know many women?'

Elaine Chambers was interviewed for fifteen hours on one day and nine on a subsequent day by a sergeant-major and corporal from the Royal Military Police.

'I had been called in by my colonel on the Friday and told that the police were going to be involved. I assumed that they would not start until the Monday, and I went back to my room and put everything that could be viewed as incriminating into two bags and left them on my bed, intending to give them to a friend to look after during the investigation. Unfortunately the police came that afternoon and searched my room. I never even thought to say no and ask for a lawyer — you just assume that they can do whatever they want. They put on latex gloves and spent three hours going through my one small room looking for evidence that I was gay. It was all in the two bags on my bed. There were three video tapes without labels and they wanted to know what was on them. I said that it was Victoria Wood and a James Dean film and they put them on to check. It was as though they thought I would have a *Lusty Lesbians Ravage Dogs in the Desert* film there.

'They read all my personal letters in front of me, which was utterly humiliating. They made no list of what they'd taken. When they interviewed me for fifteen hours on the Monday they wanted to know everything about what I'd done in bed with everyone and about the allegations of indecent assault on two particular women. Both of them had been put in a position where they either had to say I had forced them into a situation, or admit that they were lesbian. Fortunately one of them had the strength, once she had seen what was happening, to tell our colonel, the commanding officer, and then the police, that she had not been assaulted but that what had happened had been voluntary and consensual. She was a high-flying captain about to start a prestigious training course, and was heterosexual. She was a good friend and it turned out had initiated our encounter out of curiosity about lesbians. I think that she was feeling guilty anyway, but the investigation and "outing" caused her to have a nervous breakdown and she was evacuated to hospital in Britain before being medically discharged on psychiatric grounds.'

Elaine admitted that she was gay, but when asked to name others refused, saying that they had already ruined her career, why should she help them to ruin other people's? But from Elaine's letters the Royal Military Police were able to identify a sergeant in Hong Kong with fifteen years' service; a warrant officer, who was the sergeant's former partner with eighteen years' service, and Elaine's first lover from before she was Commissioned, a lance-corporal staff nurse. They were all discharged.

Once officials and investigators have proved that you're gay, their attitude often mellows – people make positive comments like Brett's commander and Simon's investigator. In Elaine's case her boss asked the police to stop the investigations when she saw how serious it was becoming.

However, despite investigating officers' personal feelings, and the support many men and women on their way out receive from officers and colleagues, all these people lose their jobs – and suffer emotionally and often financially for many years.

Men and women like Simon Ingram, Elaine Chambers or Brett Burnell say that they are not looking for any special consideration or privilege; they are certainly not looking for positive discrimination. But at present, they explain, they do not possess the right to be judged on the same criteria as their peers. The qualities of reliability, leadership, common sense and obedience that the military value highly are not the exclusive preserve of heterosexual men and women.

What makes a good serviceman or woman is a capacity for doing the job well, and there is no argument that sexual choice has anything to do with this aptitude. Nevertheless, however good lesbians or gay men are at their jobs, there are no circumstances in which they will be allowed to continue their careers in the armed forces.

In recent years Ian Waterhouse, Elaine Chambers, Simon Ingram, Brett Burnell, and Sam Waters have all found themselves suddenly out in the real world looking for work. 'It felt pretty stupid going into the Job Centre and explaining that I was qualified to hunt submarines from an aeroplane – apparently there's not a great deal of demand for that in civilian life,' Simon says.

Although he knew he was being sacked because of the damage his presence could do to morale and discipline, Ian Waterhouse stayed at work and lived in an RAF accommodation block for seven months before he was finally allowed to find another job.

Most administrative tasks in the armed forces are complicated and sacking is no exception. There are procedures and forms and reports and hearings and then, after all that has been completed, it is time to wait. Hurry up and wait. It takes months of waiting to be told that you are definitely going to be discharged – despite the fact that this is inevitable for lesbians and gays. Finally you are given a date, and that is the day when you have to hand in your identity card and complete a 'leaving routine', to check that everything that should be handed back (like gas masks), has been, and that all the appropriate paperwork, like re-signing the Official Secrets Act, has been filled in.

At the end of this period you become a civilian. On top of the emotional trauma and depression that you have probably suffered from, this is now the time to find somewhere to live and some means of paying for it, and something to do with your life. The first port of call for most is the Unemployment Benefit Office.

Since 1991 men and women administratively discharged in this way have been generally, though not always, allowed to claim their full range of severance benefits in the shape of Re-settlement Grants and gratuities, and the Department of Social Security has allowed people to sign on for the full entitlement to Unemployment Benefit. But before 1991 the Department of Social Security often viewed a sacking for homosexuality in a very negative light and would try to withhold benefit or reduce it for a period.

The positive aspect of this reversal of fortune for many men and women is the possibility of finally being honest about themselves to others. It seems to become a time of personal development and reflection; whilst serving, few of the men and women interviewed for this book had really had a chance to sit down and talk about 'coming out', about the way in which being gay affected their emotions and feelings.

At the time of his dismissal Simon Ingram talked very lucidly about his coming out to himself. 'Retrospectively I guess it's easy to say that I always knew I was gay. My first sexual experience was at prep school when I was about ten with another boy, but to be honest I don't really think that's unusual. When I was seventeen and eighteen, and just before I joined the RAF when I was nineteen, I was having a kind of detached relationship with another boy. We had sex, of sorts, but never spoke about it. I always believed I would be able to give it up whenever I wanted to. I assumed I would just stop and go and get married and have children and stuff. Before I joined the RAF I had never met an "out" gay man and so had no role model or culture to evaluate myself against. I certainly did not consider myself to be gay.'

Brett Burnell was visiting public cruising areas when he was in his early teens, but he still wouldn't have classed himself as gay. 'I thought that queers wore dresses,' he said.

Elaine Chambers did not identify as gay when she joined, although she says that retrospectively she should have realised that she was attracted to women.

But while waiting to be thrown out, or sitting at home unemployed shortly afterwards, all these individuals had a chance to think through what had happened to them, and how they ended up in that situation in the first place.

Was it their own fault for lying about their sexuality from an early stage? Remember that the large majority of men and women in the armed forces have joined during their teenage years; for many it is their first experience of life after leaving home. A number of key questions are asked by the armed forces at the initial interview and one of them is about homosexuality. Simon Ingram was asked whether or not he knew that it was illegal to be a homosexual in the forces. He said yes. Then they asked him if he was a homosexual, and he said, he thought honestly, no.

Like many others, Simon 'came out' to himself after he joined, three years into his career. When he was twenty-one he met another man while he was on holiday in France and fell in love. That experience, although they never slept together, was enough to 'out' Simon to himself. 'I was in tears when I left and when I got back to England. I could hardly deny to myself that I was gay when I was clearly feeling so deeply for this guy. But of course, although I knew I was gay, I could not discuss my private life with anyone properly and I bottled up emotions all the time.'

Men and women in the armed forces have to 'come out' alone. The process of accepting one's own homosexuality can be difficult enough in a civilian world that is often hostile to lesbians and gay men, but to go through the process in private, amongst friends and colleagues who use the word 'queer' (along with 'black' and 'woman') as a standard term of abuse, can be a profoundly alienating experience. It is not easy to explore one's sexual identity while serving in establishments or ships with limited periods of leave; living alongside other members of the armed forces in barracks or married quarters; trying to talk to a medical service that has no duty of confidentiality to the patient; confiding in a priest who has a duty to tell your commanding officer that you've admitted being lesbian or gay; knowing that the possession of a gay book, newspaper or magazine would spell the end of your career. It is a difficult environment in which to try to understand one's own homosexuality.

When new recruits arrive at their first training establishment they are often confronted by an angry and aggressive parade training instructor marching around with his pace stick shouting about queers and fairies. Although it would be wrong to suggest that the armed forces are composed entirely of homophobic sergeant-majors, it is certainly true that new young recruits initially see the military's harshest face. It is some time before they get to be a part of the supportive community that is also part of the character of the armed forces. But even that supportive community does not appear to offer a liberal attitude to homosexuality.

The Ministry of Defence has recognised that this is the case since 1994, and the new Guidelines, in their appendix entitled, 'Instruction for the Guidance of Medical Officers in Dealing with Cases of Homosexuality where No Offence Has Been Committed' state:

> When, on the other hand, an individual admits to homosexual feelings in the first instance to a medical officer, the individual should also be warned that, notwithstanding medical confidentiality, the medical officer has a duty to report to the Commanding Officer any information relating to a serious offence, or matters which might adversely affect the health, security or discipline of the unit. If the Medical Officer is satisfied that the individual is experiencing homosexual feelings then it would be most unusual not to discuss the matter with the Commanding Officer (again if possible having obtained the individual's consent). The Medical Officer should remember that 'coming out' can be highly stressful, particularly because of the prospect of the loss of a Service career, and attention should be paid to assessment of the individual's mental state since some individuals are vulnerable to thoughts of self harm at this time.

The Royal College of Psychiatrists and the British Medical Association have both made public statements about the importance of a smooth 'coming out' for lesbians and gay men, and the psychological problems that can be associated with self-denial. The distressing nature of the 'outing' of some young men and women like the army captain who had a breakdown after Elaine's investigation shows how bad the effects can be. And even for those young people with a supportive environment to fall back into, the process can be very hard work psychologically – though the outcome is not necessarily all bad. Brett, speaking several months after his 'outing' but before his discharge said, 'I was surprised how supportive my family were, and I have never felt so relaxed about myself. I still get really depressed about it all – but not about being gay.'

Simon had similar feelings: 'The last few months, since I was 'outed' have been a freeing experience in many ways. I have been able to say that I am interested in drawing, painting and all types of art. I never dared to be interested in "arty" things before, I always thought that would give me away. I've even started crying at films, something I never did before. It's as though I have been storing up my emotions and now they are all trying to come out at once.'

But these young people, now assured in their sexuality and living lives as civilians, only represent the standard model – the straightforward 'other ranks' dismissal for homosexuality.

Fortunately Brett Burnell, Elaine Chambers, Ian Waterhouse, Sam Waters and Simon Ingram have all found the world around them supportive and have found other things to do with their lives. They are all still angry and depressed from time to time – particularly when I asked them to think back and relive their experiences – but in some ways they have been the lucky ones.

2

THE DIFFICULT LIFE OF A WOMAN

WHEN THE SEXUAL Offences Act was passed in 1864 legend has it that Queen Victoria, refusing to accept that women 'did that sort of thing' struck them out before giving the Royal Assent to the legislation. For that reason women have never been able to commit the majority of homosexual offences in Britain: in the eyes of the law lesbians do not exist.

The armed forces do not face this problem because they can always charge a lesbian woman with offences of general misconduct. The general guidelines on homosexuality in the armed forces apply equally to servicewomen and men, and, theoretically the procedures are identical. The current policy makes no distinction between discharges for men and women, describing both as 'homosexuals' throughout.

In fact women are far more seriously affected by the ban than men – in that all women, irrespective of whether or not they are actually gay, are constantly under suspicion simply because of the job that they do.

The stereotype of a successful woman in a military environment is that of a tough masculine dyke. A woman who climbs and swings well on assault courses, gives loud and clear orders on a parade ground and wears a uniform is clearly giving off confusing signals when society expects women to present themselves in quite a different way.

For men the opposite is the case. The more successful a man's military career, the further he moves away from society's stereotype of the limp-wristed effeminate homosexual. Simply by being a military man he is giving off signals that mark him out as heterosexual.

The problem for women in the armed forces is complicated even further by the male military sex ethic: is she screwable? As Army Lieutenant Elaine Chambers explains, 'You either sleep with the boys or they think you must be a dyke or one frigid bitch.'

'Unit bicycle' and 'platoon groundsheet' are two of the epithets awarded by the army to 'shaggable' women. Any heterosexual woman would probably want to avoid the advances of the kind of men who view women in this way, but by rejecting an advance – in the military environment – she will be opening herself up to the suggestion that she must be homosexual.

All servicewomen face this dilemma: the service police investigators seem to spend a disproportionately large amount of time investigating suspicions of female homosexuality when women only make up a relatively small proportion of the armed forces. Several of the women I spoke to said that they had been investigated many times in their careers. Women are more likely than their male colleagues to keep diaries and letters, and this results in the witch-hunt 'daisy-chain' investigations which periodically extend tentacle-like throughout the armed forces as the investigators work their way through name after name.

Julie and Bea, two young lesbians, were discharged from the Royal Navy in the summer of 1994 after Special Investigation Branch started one of these investigations. Julie recalls what happened.

'We were both Wrens; I joined in 1990, and Bea had joined in 1989 – we met while working together. I already thought of myself as a lesbian, but it was Bea's first relationship with a woman. We started living together and now own our own house in Portsmouth.

'A couple of years ago we were investigated and interviewed by SIB, but both denied that anything was going on. They had nothing to prove that we were together, and so we were given a warning.'

The personal property searches and interrogations took the customary form.

'In September 1990, late one evening, I was hauled out of Wrens' Quarters to a conference room in the large training and administration building by my chief Wren, and two members of the SIB. They cautioned me and told me I was being investigated for being an alleged lesbian. They questioned me at length for about two weeks. They searched all of my belongings and tore my Mess apart, seizing various letters, postcards and posters, none of which had any evidence on them at all, or contained any photographs of any explicit nature. During this investigation I received threats of discharge from the Royal Navy from my divisional officer, warrant officer, and chief Wren. None of them gave me any support or divisional backing at all. All the questioning was about one other Wren in particular, but they also mentioned several other "known lesbians" including a leading Wren who had helped me back to the Mess one night when I was drunk. They wanted to know what we had got up to on the way.

'They never specified what evidence they had to substantiate the allegations they were making.'

Bea and Julia found that coping with being a lesbian in the armed forces became very difficult. They both started drinking. Julie recalls: 'I took to drinking a lot, mainly to try and relieve the stress of "coming out". I was nineteen years old, had only just admitted to myself that I was gay, and had just gone through the worst experience of my life. My friends wouldn't speak to me and superiors treated me like a criminal. A week or so later I returned to the base after a night out and was charged for having alcohol in my room (a bottle of beer which was nearly empty) and got seven days' "nines" (extra duties and stoppage of leave).

'Bea had a similar problem in October. We were trying to come to terms with our feelings for each other, our feelings about ourselves and our feelings about the navy.

'It was after all this had happened that we went away together for a weekend in Southampton and the relationship began. Until then we had just been close friends.'

As the relationship between them strengthened, so did their

ability to perform at work. Both of them had experienced disciplinary problems – mostly involving alcohol – whilst they were trying to sort out their personal lives. But the stability of a relationship was reflected in their improved evaluations. By the time they were discharged Bea was about to be promoted to the rank of leading Wren. But the spectre of another investigation was always just around the corner. There was also the problem that one of their NCOs seemed to take pleasure in rooting out and reporting suspected lesbians. There have been several cases where individual men and women who have a particularly strong fear of homosexuals make a habit of informing on those whom they suspect.

Army Lieutenant Elaine Chambers found that the woman who had started the investigation in Germany was a lesbian herself, who felt that she needed to prove her heterosexuality in order to gain promotion. Perhaps that is what happened when Julie's and Bea's NCO started reporting everyone she suspected; whatever the case may be she has been commended by the SIB for her diligence.

It was 1991 and nearly a year since their last investigation: it was time for another 'witch-hunt' at HMS *Dryad*. Bea recalls: 'The first I knew of the SIB being in the Wrens' quarters was when they barged past me on their way to search Kate's room – another lesbian Wren who was having a relationship with an officer. The next thing I knew about was when I was asked if I had anything to tell the SIB about a relationship I was having. I said no and left.

'A couple of days later I came back to the Mess for lunch and to meet Julie, and a leading Wren told me that Julie was with the SIB. I saw Julie and an RPO Wren [policewoman] in the lift in the Wrens' quarters and started to chat to her. The RPO Wren looked at us and told us not to speak to each other. We left and I went to my room and put a CD on full blast. I thought that I was bound to be called in but I wasn't that night, so when Julie came back we went out and collaborated on our story. I scribbled over letters and postcards in my room, and cut pages out of my diaries.

'The next day I was hauled in and questioned and then it

was my turn to have things turned upside down. It was around five pm when they came to my room, and everyone on my side of the floor had to be turfed out. I had to take down all my pictures, cards and photos, and there were lots, and they tipped my drawers out and emptied my wardrobe. They looked through all my photo albums and took all my letters and diaries going back seven years. In the end I got upset and threw my books at them. Then they marched me over to the administration building and continued questioning me. By this time everybody was in the dining hall having tea, and they could all see what was going on as I was marched off with my belongings. It was the most humiliating thing that has happened to me. I was questioned further, but they had no evidence and it just ended.'

Although these investigations may end for the SIB, for a while the individual man or woman under suspicion – many of whom are, of course, not homosexual – has to live with the gossip and rumour that investigations such as this generate. Bea moved to a different job at a different base, and found when she got there that her reputation had preceded her. This time the tension was with men rather than women.

'Everyone knew about the investigation. I worked mainly with lads and at times they could be worse than women. I offered to babysit for one lad and he said yes, but added that he didn't want his daughter saying that I'd touched her when he came home. I broke down and my new chief had words with everyone.'

Julie had gone through a similarly humiliating investigation: 'They questioned me about where we went together outside the base, where we went at weekends together, whether we slept in the same rooms and whether we had a sexual relationship. They searched my room and seized boxes full of letters, diaries, postcards, photos and everything. I had known it was coming after they took Kate away for questioning – she had been asked about us. They searched through my chequebook stubs and came across the name of a bed and breakfast in Southampton, which was where our relationship had started. They went down to the guest house and took a statement from the landlady and examined the room which we had stayed in. Unfortunately for them it had three beds in it and they couldn't prove anything with that. We both got a bit sick of it all and called in the duty solicitors. As soon as they were involved the SIB seemed to stop the investigation.'

Julie had decided that she wanted to leave the Royal Navy anyway, and had put in her required eighteen months' notice by the end of 1993. Over the following months Bea found the stability of the relationship reassuring, and was about to be promoted to leading Wren. Then everything finally fell apart.

The premature end of their careers in the Royal Navy came as an indirect result of the bitterness felt by a former colleague, Cathy, who had been caught by the SIB herself a couple of years earlier – and had lost her own job. Cathy knew both Julie and Bea, and had remained in touch. Early in 1993 Cathy phoned Julie from Germany, where she was staying with her parents, to say that she was coming to look for a job in Portsmouth and asked if she could stay with them while she went to interviews.

'She wanted to stay with us, but we didn't feel too happy about her being around us that much since we were at risk all the time. We only have two bedrooms in the house and having a known lesbian stay would have raised questions. We talked to her over the phone a couple of times and I brought the conversation around to a friend of ours who was also in the navy, who we knew was lonely at the time and had a spare room. We gave Cathy the phone number of our friend, and didn't hear from either of them for a week afterwards. By the time we did Cathy was practically moving in with our friend. They had a relationship and our friend helped Cathy to get a job. Everything was going OK until they started having arguments about Cathy's lack of contribution to the bills, and Cathy also put a lot of pressure on our friend to make her go out to bars and clubs, which would have been very risky for her. Our friend was all too aware of the consequences of doing something so stupid. After having her freedom for so long and not having to hide, Cathy just did her own thing and left our friend to it.

'One day, whilst I was at work, I got a phone call from our friend, she was in the Royal Navy's hospital at Haslar. Cathy had had a blazing row with her, and had beaten her up quite badly. She had a broken nose, a black eye, bruised ribs and everything. She was terrified of being asked about her injuries.'

If Julie's and Bea's friend had done the right thing and reported the assault to the police, she would have lost her own job. Julie helped her come up with a story about a fight outside a pub to explain away the injuries. Most important of all she wanted to get Cathy out of the house.

'When I got home from work with Bea we got a phone call. Our friend had locked Cathy out of the house and put all her items into black bin bags in the street. She had not put her stereo system out as well, and Cathy was trying to smash the front door down to get it. Our friend wanted payment for her outstanding bills before handing it over. We could hear the commotion in the background and told her to stay where she was and that we'd get to her as soon as we could. When we got there a police sergeant was with Cathy outside the house, trying to calm her down. Cathy tried to speak to us, but we went in to see if our friend was all right. Her face was a complete mess where Cathy had assaulted her. The sergeant said that if they could come to an arrangement then he'd let it all go. Our friend said that she wouldn't press charges for assault and that Cathy could have her stereo back, if Cathy wrote a cheque for the money that she owed her. The sergeant made sure that all this happened, and then Cathy left with all her things.'

Cathy, knowing how the system works, and obviously embittered, went to see the SIB at HMS *Nelson* in Portsmouth and told them everything – and named Bea and Julie in her statement. As a former Wren herself she knew exactly what she was doing – and the investigations began again.

Julie was called in for a long interview and said 'No comment' to all the questions. Bea answered their questions, but said that they were not gay and were just sharing the house for financial reasons. It is quite normal in this situation for the

SIB to lie about what one suspect has said in order to persuade the other that the game is up: this is an illegal practice, but one which continues. (Two RAF officers who were investigated in 1994 in Scotland were caught out in this way when one was told that the other had already confessed.)

Julie was not really shaken by what happened – she had after all put in her notice to leave the Navy in a year's time.

'I had decided to leave, and was not really that unhappy about it. But Bea did not want to leave – she was just about to be promoted to leading Wren. My captain said that it would simply be easier for me to leave a bit earlier than I would have done otherwise and I went job-hunting with this understanding – but then, just a few days before I was supposed to go, I was called in and told that I could not leave on the earlier date, but had to wait for the original one. They insisted that I stayed at work for another two weeks because, they said, I had to leave on their terms, not mine. I had already found a new job and I nearly lost it because I was not able to start when they wanted me to – I told the Navy that, and they just said "tough".'

Julie and Bea were both discharged, although ultimately neither had admitted that they were lesbian. They both made representations complaining about their discharges, which were unsuccessful, and they are both now contemplating legal action against the Royal Navy for wrongful dismissal.

Throughout the 1980s Britain and the United States followed the same pattern of investigation: search and seizure of letters and diaries, the collection of names and statements, and ultimately the interview of more and more women. Michelle Benecke of the Service Members' Legal Defense Network in Washington DC analysed this problem in a paper on the subject written with Kirstin Dodge:

A wave of anti-lesbian investigations swept through ships and military installations. These included investigations on the USS *Norton Sound*, resulting in the discharge of eight women sailors in 1980; the hospital ship *Sanctuary* and the USS *Dixon*; the army's ouster of eight female military police officers from the US Military Academy at West Point in 1986;

the investigation of thirty women, including every African-American woman, on board the destroyer-tender USS *Yellowstone*, which resulted in the discharge of eight women; and the 1988 investigation of five of the thirteen female crewmembers on board the USS *Grapple*. One of the most infamous investigations took place at the Marine recruitment installation at Parris Island, South California, where over half the 246 women at the base were questioned about alleged homosexual activities. Sixty-five women were eventually discharged or chose to resign or accept voluntary discharges rather than face extensive investigations, the possibility of criminal charges, and the emotional and financial costs of salvaging their careers. Three women were actually imprisoned for engaging in homosexual activities.

Lesbian women in the armed forces seem to form close networks and friendships with others and then keep in touch as they move from unit to unit. This is not so evident among gay men who are often surprised to find out that a colleague, or former colleague, is gay. During the research for this book I have been able to 'break' it to a number of men that a former colleague of theirs is also gay. Women seem to know already. Yvonne, a serving officer in the British army, was told by gay friends in one unit who she should meet and go out with when she got to her next establishment. Perhaps this is why, once the investigators have found out the identity of one lesbian woman, they will spend such extraordinary amounts of time and money trying to root out others. The idea of military policemen visiting boarding houses in seaside resorts to count the number of beds in the rooms in order to work out who could have slept where is really quite bizarre.

Caroline Meaghr had been in the Royal Military Police for thirteen years by 1990 when she lost her job because she was suspected of being a lesbian. Part of her job had been to spot gay women. 'We were told to look at their pictures and record collections. Anyone with Joan Armatrading records was immediately suspect.'

The service police know the language and the locations that make up a part of the gay community in their area. Julie and Bea feel able to visit the gay pub Drummonds in Portsmouth now – but they know that the SIB visit it in plain clothes from time to time to have a look. Former Seaman Brett Burnell met an on-duty RPO from the SIB at HMS *Nelson* in that pub in 1993.

In the wake of the Gulf War *The Times* journalist Kate Muir wrote a book about the role of women in the armed forces, and how it had changed over the years to a position where Operation Desert Storm could not have happened without its women soldiers, sailors and air force personnel. From air defence missile batteries to engineering on board ships in the Gulf, from running transport and ammunition to and from the front line to managing hospitals at the front with the constant threat of SCUD missile and chemical attack – women are now completely integrated into the military machine.

Yet these women still have to tread the fine line between femininity and 'dyke-like' military professionalism. It is often their rejection of male interest, or their failure to cope well with a heterosexual relationship of convenience that results in their downfall. The following story appeared in the *Harvard Women's Law Journal*, volume 13, in spring 1990:

> In July 1988, twenty-three-year-old Corporal Barbara Baum, a military policewoman, was convicted by a general court martial of sodomy, seven counts of indecency, and conspiracy to obstruct justice. The charges against Baum arose from information provided to investigators by Baum's former lover, Lance-Corporal Diana Maldonado, in exchange for a grant of testimonial immunity. Baum was sentenced to one year in jail, demotion to Private, and a dishonorable discharge.
>
> The briefest affair between Baum and Maldonado was discovered by Maldonado's spurned boyfriend in October 1986 when he kicked in the door of their motel room and found them naked in bed together. An investigation of the women was not immediately initiated, however, because of the boyfriend's lack of perceived credibility.
>
> Over a year later, Baum, *en route* to an assignment in Hawaii, was recalled for questioning. Military officials believed that she could provide information to agents conducting an investigation of alleged lesbian activities among female drill instructors at Parris Island. Baum's refusal to

co-operate with investigators contributed to the military pro-
secutor's decision to try her case by general court martial,
even though it involved no allegation of assault. This decision
sent a strong message to other Marines to co-operate in the investigation.

Maldonado's account of oral sex with Baum on the night of
the motel incident led to the charge of sodomy against Baum.
Explicit questioning of Maldonado at Baum's trial provided
sufficient evidence to prove the necessary elements of the
sodomy offense. Maldonado also admitted to 'passionate kissing and fondling of genitalia' between her and Baum at
Baum's residence and gave uncorroborated testimony that
Baum had told her of Baum's other physical contact with
women during a game of 'truth and dare' at a party in May
1986.

In June 1988, three weeks after her imprisonment, Baum
succumbed to agents' promises of clemency and an upgraded
discharge if she co-operated in the ongoing investigation of
women Marines. During fourteen hours of questioning, she
gave investigators the names of over seventy-seven women she
knew, or suspected to be homosexual. Baum served 226 days
of her one year sentence before being released from the military prison at Quantico, Virginia.

In theory the situation in the United States has changed,
making these types of investigation more difficult. But that is
not the case in Britain. The Royal Military Police, Royal
Navy Special Investigations Branch, and the RAF Provost and
Security Service actively investigate, pursue and carry out surveillance to find lesbians and gay men – and lesbians seem to
take up a surprisingly large proportion of their time.

Kate Muir, when researching for her book, was surprised
how large a proportion of the women she met were lesbians.
Is there something about the military life that attracts gay
women? Elaine Chambers thinks that is probably true.

'As gay women the stereotypical view is that we should all
be working in the forces, or the police, or the prison service,
or in hospitals. There is something about an ordered female
life that is attractive to gay women, and I think that for once
the stereotypes are right. In the population at large there are
not that many lesbians, statistically, but when I was in the

army there were lots of us. I wouldn't say we were in the majority or anything like that, but there are a hell of a lot of us – in every area, every hospital, every unit. Maybe we are naturally good at being in the military, the armed forces here would come to a complete standstill if they actually succeeded in throwing out all the gay women there are.

'For the most part the gay and straight women integrate well. You can basically know soon after joining who is and who isn't, but no one really makes an issue out of it. Some straight women don't mind at all and are really relaxed about it. Some don't like it at all, but there's a sense of live and let live and if you keep your sexuality pretty much to yourself, even the women who don't like it would do nothing to drop you into trouble. In my case it was another gay woman looking for promotion.

'When I went to the office in Britain to be finally thrown out there were several women officers there who worked for the boss. One of them was the girlfriend of the woman major who started all the investigations into me – she knew that I knew who she was and looked terrified as I went in to be sacked. Of course I didn't say anything, but it just goes to show how stupid it all is. We are everywhere, and if we're good at our job we should be left alone to do it.'

Caroline Meaghr, who was a staff sergeant in the Royal Military Police, is well aware of the lengths that she and her colleagues used to go to catch lesbians:

'There would be a very detailed search of their possessions. We would read every letter. We would look everywhere for evidence. This would be followed by very long interviews – two to three hours at a time.

'It was never enough for somebody to confess – we then had to prove that they were gay. That meant detailed descriptions of how they had sex, and with whom.'

She remembers that eventually most of the women they interviewed gave in and spoke honestly about themselves.

'I sat there a few times and I wanted to say, "Don't answer these questions". But it is a rank thing and the interviewers are male sergeants and staff sergeants and the women felt obliged to answer.'

She confirms that, like Elaine Chambers's investigation which went half-way round the world to Hong Kong, many involve questioning in several countries. She was also aware of surveillance operations that were carried out – in particular following women from an army base to see which pubs they went to. More alarmingly, Caroline Meaghr recalls the setting up of what she calls a 'lesbian index' within the Royal Military Police records office: 'Everyone who had ever been mentioned during an investigation, even if they were just friends on the fringes would be named. If their name was on the index the investigator could use it to bully the woman – it might intimidate somebody into confessing. I left four years ago, but it is probably still in existence.'

She is right in her assumption that the lesbian index does still exist, although in fact, the office that compiles it also keeps an index of the names of suspected gay men as well.

In a Royal Military Police report on an army private, who was subsequently sacked, written in July 1994, SIB investigators state, 'A CCRIO check in this case proved negative.'

What, I wanted to know, was a CCRIO check? Could it be the index which Caroline Meaghr was talking about? I asked the Ministry of Defence, who explained that the acronym stands for the Central Criminal Records Index Office. It is a database run by the Royal Military Police to which all the other service police forces have access. It also provides information to the civilian police.

According to the Ministry of Defence the CCRIO stores information on all investigations carried out by the service police – whether or not they result in criminal charges or convictions. It is a criminal intelligence resource which can be used to cross-refer between different inquiries and agencies.

I asked the Ministry of Defence specifically whether the CCRIO holds information on the sex life of members of the armed forces. It was emphasised to me in response that the CCRIO holds names and data relating to *all* investigations. This clearly includes the investigations into sexuality that occupy a great deal of service police time. Caroline Meaghr is accurate in her accusation that the RMP keep a 'lesbian index'.

Since the 1984 Data Protection Act was passed, all computer databases that store personal information have had to be registered with the Data Protection Registrar. As part of the registration process the database owner has to specify what categories of information he keeps and with whom he shares it.

The Ministry of Defence appears to be in contravention of the Data Protection Act in its register entry. The MOD has specified that it keeps information for police purposes on its database – and that it shares that information with other police forces and a range of other organisations including the British Telecom intelligence department and Post Office investigations department.

However, the Ministry of Defence does not register the fact that it keeps information on an individual's sex life for police purposes. The category for this type of information is listed by the Data Protection Registrar as type 'C115' – the Ministry acknowledge that they keep 'C115' information for security vetting purposes in another entry, but the 'policing' entry is specific that information on sex life is not stored. This appears to contradict the Ministry's own statement on the nature of the information stored by the CCRIO.

The references to the British Telecom intelligence department, and the Post Office investigations department are relevant to Caroline Meaghr: she was interviewed after her letters had been intercepted, and was accused of having a relationship with a senior officer. As a policewomen she found herself on the other side of the fence.

'I did have some letters which were fairly explicit. I was denied access to a lawyer. They told me that they would not court-martial me and I had to put my notice in. It was made clear I should leave the army.' As she was working in Northern Ireland she had an important job which she was not able to hand over properly to a replacement. She still feels angry about the way that she was hounded out.

Karen Brown, a navy rating, and her girlfriend in the RAF lost their jobs in 1992 after the SIB and the RAF P&SS had used the techniques that Caroline Meaghr describes to investigate them.

'Although they have a list of people they suspect of being gay, they couldn't prove that we were lesbians. They need a confession or definite proof, and as we both refused to declare ourselves, the investigation went on hold, but my girlfriend got transferred to a base in Norwich. We wanted to be together so I'd travel up every weekend to be with her. Then her base started to keep a note of how many times my car was parked there. And they must have been following us because they knew when we'd been to Great Yarmouth together.

'It all came to a head in August 1991. I came back from Norwich one weekend and they'd intercepted a letter from a friend which made suggestive comments about me being gay. The cross-examinations started again, only worse this time. The SIB confronted me about the trips to Yarmouth and Norwich. My girlfriend's cross-examination was even worse, she nearly cracked up.'

Karen Brown and her girlfriend were both fed up with the pressure of investigation, and being under surveillance, and they decided to confess.

'Then they questioned us about what we did together in bed, how many times did we do it and what fingers and other things we used on each other. The whole episode was so disgusting, they were like perverts. They enjoyed asking and told us we couldn't refuse to tell them. I was nearly sick. The RAF investigators were even harder on my girlfriend.

'We remained on our bases while they completed the investigation, which took a few months. Then we got our discharge dates. Until then we were not allowed to work in security-sensitive posts, despite being highly trained. I gave out passes until I left and she worked on the telephone switchboard. By this time gossip had got around and some of the other service people were horrible to us. I was formally discharged from the navy in January 1991, and my girlfriend was discharged a couple of weeks later. We were both devastated because we had lost our careers and our homes, we had nothing left. I was lucky because I had served more than my three-year minimum so people thought that I'd left voluntarily, but my girlfriend hadn't, so her leaving looked suspicious. Even my parents don't know the truth about my dismissal. After this we moved into a terrible flat above a shop and eventually got new jobs.'

Just like dozens of other men and women, Karen and her partner want to challenge the Ministry of Defence in court over their dismissals – after all, their sexuality aside, they had superb records.

'I've been in touch with Rank Outsiders and Stonewall and I've got myself a solicitor who's looking at the best way of taking my case to the European courts. I hope all the dismissed service people can take their cases there because it still makes me so angry and annoyed when I think about the way we were treated by the armed forces. All I ever wanted to do was be in the navy and it was the same for my girlfriend. To be honest, even if I was offered my old job back tomorrow, things would never be the same again. I've lost my enthusiasm for everything.'

Other women are fighting their dismissals too. Senior Aircraftwoman Jeanette Smithe from RAF Halton in Berkshire is intending to take action after an investigation carried out while she was on leave in June 1994 proved that she was gay: 'My friend had left a message on the answerphone telling me that my tutors had found out that I was gay. I was stunned because over the past five years I'd never had any problems whatsoever. I reported to the deputy matron in Halton, and was interviewed by my tutor. He asked me if the allegations were true, and I said that they were. I was then interviewed by the military police – but I wasn't charged with anything.'

The police also interviewed her civilian partner, and she has to wait for a dismissal date.

'The reference that I have to offer people will tell people that my services in the Royal Air Force were no longer required. My career is ruined because I haven't finished my training yet. I have no civil rights.'

In terms of civil rights, men and women face the same obstacles when trying to defend their right to serve as lesbians or gay men. But the nature of military culture itself discriminates against lesbian women serving with even more vehemence than it does men.

3

DAMAGE LIMITATION

IN THE CURRENT economic climate the loss of a job, from time to time, may be regarded as an inevitable part of working life. But for most of their members the armed forces are more than just a nine-to-five job; military service is both a vocation and an entire way of life. In much the same way as a boarding school builds up a twenty-four-hour a day routine for children, the armed forces create a whole way of life for adults. People who join up live together, play together, and their children and wives do likewise. If they are thrown out of this community they have to start all over again from the very beginning.

Throughout the 1980s and 1990s coal mines have been closed, mining communities have suffered terribly and have had to find a new *raison d'être*, a new direction – but at least the miners were not sent to prison first. Even if British Coal no longer has a job for each former miner, it will at least give them references as they search for further employment. Try that if your employer simply says that you were court-martialled for gross indecency, imprisoned and dismissed; which happened as recently as 1985.

For some men and women, leaving the armed forces may be no bad thing: after the initial shock and re-evaluation has taken place, many find another job or profession that offers them great satisfaction. While they wouldn't condone the discriminatory laws and regulations that saw them dismissed, they would cheerfully acknowledge that they are now happy in other walks of life. David, an army bomb-disposal expert, joined the police force after he resigned in 1992, and former RAF Sergeant Simon Ingram has become a television researcher. Not everyone is able to adapt so quickly to a new way of life; in fact most of the men and women interviewed for this book said that, given the opportunity, they would seriously consider rejoining. Only a handful said they were happier with their work now than they were before they left the armed forces. The majority of those discharged for homosexuality find their lives in complete turmoil for a long time. Most said that they had been able to sort out their emotional lives more easily outside the service environment. But any positive emotional side to the dismissal has to be seen alongside the potential effects of the loss of home, friends and social life. Individuals who have lost their jobs usually have to cope with a major drop in income and living standards as well.

Royal Navy seaman Brett Burnell spent six months on the dole, and a year after his discharge was still working in a very low-paid job and staying temporarily in a series of friends' flats. Mike Sansom was discharged from the RAF in 1992, and worked as a guard for a series of private security companies – he described it as 'dead-end work'. – before beginning training as a nursing assistant in 1994. His salary at the time he was dismissed was £14,500 a year – two years later he was earning £7,000.

For some the loss of their career has much wider implications and their lives are profoundly changed by the current regulations.

Flight-Lieutenant Steve Purvis left the RAF under a cloud in 1985 after thirteen years' service. He was court-martialled for gross indecency after admitting that he was involved in a consensual relationship with an RAF corporal.

'I joined the Royal Air Force as an apprentice when I was sixteen and went to RAF Cosford to train in communications, radar, and navigation instruments, but when I failed an exam on communications I retrained on an adult course (I was eighteen then), concentrating on instruments. I passed the exams and went to my first job as a technician on Vulcan bombers at RAF Waddington.'

Steve Purvis applied for a commission as an officer, and after he was accepted started his pilot training. Six months later he proved unsuccessful as a pilot and then went to the RAF College at Cranwell to qualify as an engineering officer. He passed this course and started his first job in the tactical communications branch at RAF Brize Norton. This job meant regular one-, two- and three-week exercises in Germany and elsewhere in Europe preparing to set up communications networks in the event of war. His next job was with 16 Squadron of the RAF Regiment (the RAF's soldiers, responsible for defending airfields), and he was in charge of the Rapier Air Defence Missiles at RAF Wildenrath in West Germany for two years.

He served two tours with Rapier units in the Falkland Islands, before appointment to his first command position in charge of RAF and Army Rapier units at RAF Rheindahlen in West Germany. It was while serving in the Falklands that he first began coming out to himself.

'I was sixteen when I joined the RAF and I had no idea I was gay then. I had girlfriends in the years in between and it was not until my late twenties that I knew I was gay. I had no choice in the matter whatsoever. It's my nature, but I knew the RAF couldn't accept it.

'It was a really demanding job which I enjoyed and I had to have pretty high security clearance for it. It was at this time that I went to dinner with a girlfriend near Brize Norton and she had invited several of her friends who were RAF stewards. There was one guy there who caught my eye immediately and we fell in love. I used to come back from Germany for weekends and spend them with him.'

They were caught out in a surprising way.

'I found out later how they got on to us – I had taken the car ferry back to Germany after seeing him, and while I was on the ferry I started talking to this young American guy who was obviously very upset about something. It turned out that he had just come out to himself and was scared to go back to his family in the States. I felt quite comfortable about my sexuality by that stage and took him to a quieter bit of the ferry to talk to him and give him some advice. He was really upset and I was holding his hand while I was talking to him. I remember someone walking past and looking at us while I sat there, and it turned out later that he was an RAF warrant officer and he reported having seen me.'

As a result of this report Steve Purvis was covertly followed on his next weekend's leave to Britain and was seen visiting the house where his partner lived. After he left his partner was arrested and questioned. One of the other RAF stewards who lived in the house telephoned Steve and told him what had happened. Shortly afterwards the RAF police called Steve into their offices. He sat and listened while the RAF policemen outlined what they believed had occurred and read chunks of his boyfriend's statement to him. The RAF policemen told Flight-Lieutenant Purvis that his boyfriend was very distraught and wanted to talk to him.

'I decided to tell the truth and started to talk to them. They didn't tape-record interviews then, and my statement ran to twenty-eight pages. They wanted to know about precisely what we had done in bed and wouldn't use phrases like "made love". They insisted on graphic anatomical descriptions which made everything sound clinical and unpleasant. I was told that if I talked openly about everything then it would be easier and, stupidly, I believed them, and named two other people I had been involved with. In the end all these bits that were supposed to help me were read out in great detail at my court martial and I was made to look like I was preying on people.'

Although his boyfriend was discharged administratively, and the other two whom he named were honourably discharged, Steve was charged and court-martialled on sixteen offences of 'gross indecency'.

'I was twenty-eight, he was twenty-four, and we were having a consensual relationship that would have been entirely legal in civilian life. It was only on the basis of our statements that they were able to list all the sixteen offences – I had given them the information myself, and since we were involved in a relationship sixteen offences were not difficult to come up with. I corroborated the statement voluntarily and was court-martialled as a result of having done so. They told me to talk to them in order to make things easier!'

In late summer 1985 Flight-Lieutenant Steve Purvis was quick-marched into a wooden floored barracks room with a table, behind which were five or six officers and a judge advocate.

'Prisoner, stand at ease.'

'Prisoner, sit down.'

Steve was defended by a civilian barrister who was surprised by the vehemence of the prosecution. He had the impression that there was a political agenda behind the judge's advocate's refusal to rule any of the evidence inadmissable. When Steve realised that if he continued to plead not guilty all the details would be heard by a *Sun* newspaper reporter who was sitting in the court room, and therefore would be read by his family and friends, he changed his plea to one of guilty to three of the charges. He could have been sentenced to two years for each of the charges, but was in the end sentenced to six months' imprisonment.

Now disgraced, Steve was sent back to Germany to the Officers' Mess, where, since there was no appropriate accommodation for convicted officers, he was held in a comfortable room while waiting to find out if the commander-in-chief would confirm his sentence. There was clearly confusion about what to do with the prisoner, and he spent the time in his room, attended by an officer of equal or higher rank. He ordered meals from the Mess menu, which were brought to his room. After a few days he complained that he was not able to get any exercise, and so he was allowed to go for runs and walks, attended by his accompanying officer. As he had been convicted he was not entitled to wear his cap and he made a point of walking past the commander-in-chief's building without his cap on – an offence of great discourtesy. He was ordered not to walk or run on that route – but every day he had a different accompanying officer, who was unaware of the rule, and Steve managed to walk past the office capless.

Steve had been convicted in September, but was still on the base waiting for a decision about his sentence in December. He began to make a fuss and demanded to know whether or not it was going to be confirmed. In the end it was, and he was sent to a civilian prison in Gloucester to complete his sentence. He was driven there by a black driver accompanied by another officer. When they arrived at the prison, the prison officers assumed that the driver was the prisoner and ordered him into another room to undress. Steve had to take charge and point out that he was the prisoner.

In his interview the next morning with the prison governor, he was offered protection as he might be thought of as a sex offender by the other prisoners. Steve maintained he had done nothing criminal and wanted to be treated normally.

'The other prisoners didn't believe I had been sent to prison for having a consensual relationship with someone practically my own age, and I had a couple of fights.'

Eventually one of the prisoners who worked in the offices looked at his file and confirmed that he had been telling the truth. After that he became a figure of interest and was asked many questions. He spent Christmas 1985 in prison.

When Steve was released his boyfriend, the now-dismissed RAF corporal, was waiting for him outside.

'We went to see my parents, but they ran a newsagent's shop and had been bombarded with the details of the whole affair. Their local paper had covered the story in great detail and they didn't know what to do or say. I didn't really have anything more to do with them. My boyfriend and I moved to Brighton – I had no money.'

He also had no job, and no reference for the previous thirteen years of his life, a criminal conviction for an offence that was not criminal in civilian life and no pension contributions or terminal benefits after thirteen years' payment and service.

'As the Rapier missile specialist in Germany I had dealings with British Aerospace, GEC, Marconi, Decca and all the big defence contractors. When I left I should have been able to work for one of them, but who was going to employ me in my specialist area? It was all denied to me.'

The only positive thing Steve really remembers from this period is the letters he received from colleagues and subordinates saying that they didn't understand why it had happened, and that he had been their best CO.

Disgraced Flight-Lieutenant Steve Purvis went on to become a commission-only double-glazing salesman in Brighton.

'I'm not angry any more, though I was for a long time. I don't think the RAF understood the long-term implications of what they were doing. I had always tried to be professional and discreet – but I might as well have slept with every steward I ever fancied, or every airman under my command. I was given no credit whatsoever for being the honest person I tried to be.'

The chain of events that affected Steve Purvis in 1985 may seem somewhat out of kilter with a Britain that was staging gay drama on the West End stage in London; a Britain where entrepreneurs were fighting to own London's biggest gay night club; a Britain which had its first mainstream gay soap-opera character, Colin, on television in *EastEnders*. But Steve's experiences were easier than the scenario confronting Peter Williams when he was thrown out of the navy in 1977.

Peter Williams had joined the Royal Navy in 1972 after two years working on the merchant fleet, and before that he had been at a navy school. He was obviously destined for a navy life, but in 1975 he realised he was gay. He made no secret of the fact – but at that time the navy still made a distinction between gay feelings and gay activity. He was reminded that homosexual activity was completely forbidden and continued to serve.

In 1977 he was working as an electrical technician on HMS *Leander*, a frigate, and was waiting for his advancement to leading seaman rate to be confirmed. The executive officer on board, a lieutenant-commander made it clear that he was opposed to the promotion on the grounds that an admitted homosexual should not have responsibility over other sailors. The case was referred to the Admiralty Board, which ordered that the promotion to leading rate should proceed, on the basis that Peter Williams was to be treated like any other rating. He was promoted to acting LREM and the executive officer complained again. As a result of this, an investigation into acting LREM Williams began.

'I had done nothing at all, except get promoted. They came and searched my locker on board and took away letters and a couple of badges. I was taken off the ship, which was in refit in Portsmouth, and taken to the cells at HMS *Nelson*. Before they locked me up they took me to their Mess and gave me a couple of large vodkas so that I would talk more easily. After some questions I was told to strip to my shorts, thrown a blanket and put in a cell. I spent three days there while they questioned me. I told them that I was gay, but I had told them that since 1975. After forty-eight hours or so they said I had to have a medical. I said that I didn't want or need one, but I was taken anyway to see a surgeon commander and a lieutenant who I later realised must have been a psychiatrist. He talked to me for a while and wanted to know if I was the active or passive partner.

'After he had spoken to me, the surgeon commander said that I had to have a medical and took me to another room, where there was a table with a paper cover. I said that I strongly objected to this. I had admitted that I was gay and did not want a medical. The surgeon commander said that I had to have one and ordered me to get undressed and get on the table. There were two prisoners' escorts with me who stayed watching, one leading regulator and another who was training. I complained, but was told that they were going to do the examination anyway.

'They opened my legs and forced an instrument into me like a large pair of silver scissors with a tube on the end that opened up and was obviously for internal examinations. The surgeon commander and another medical officer looked, prodded and discussed it. The surgeon commander invited the two leading regulators to come and look as well. It was very uncomfortable and utterly degrading.

'There was nothing much more I could say to stop them. When they had finished the surgeon commander threw me a towel and told me to get dressed. I was taken immediately back to the cell block and ordered to clean out the vans that had vomit all over them from the previous night's shore patrol. Then I was taken to the NAAFI and had to walk past two or three hundred other sailors to collect the prisoners' food. Finally I was sent back to my ship.'

Peter Williams found this his Mess had been informed of what had happened and instructed not to talk about it. He was told he was still under arrest and could not leave the ship. But the expected hassle and homophobic banter did not materialise, and his colleagues treated him normally and passed him cans of beer as he lay on his bunk – in tears at first. After two weeks he asked why he couldn't go ashore and was told, after some phone calls were made, that he could.

Eight or nine months later, while the ship was in an intensive training period at Weymouth in Dorset, the Admiralty Board's decision that he was to be discharged immediately came through. During the intervening months Peter Williams had served as a completely 'out' gay man. He had encountered no problems working with colleagues or living in the Mess and was still enjoying his job.

' "We hope you can find a suitable career in civilian life," they said to me.'

In October 1977 Peter Williams found himself standing on the station platform at Plymouth with nothing other than a rail warrant and his bags to show for his navy career.

'I went up north, back home, and stayed with my parents – who were upset that I was suddenly homeless and jobless. I didn't settle down for about five years, I just drifted into one job and then another. I worked as a clerk and in transport. I was angry with the navy, but I didn't see any real point in complaining at the time. People thought differently twenty years ago and there was no point in making a fuss. After five years I began to get my act together and set up my own company manufacturing food. It was reasonably successful and my life got some sort of order about it again.'

Patrick Lyster-Todd joined the Royal Navy in 1972, and, although his eyesight was not good enough to become a seaman officer – the only branch which can go on to command a ship – he fought and fought to transfer to the seaman branch. After training as an engineer and an air-traffic controller, he finally left the navy and re-applied, the only way he could manage to overcome the red tape and challenge the eyesight decision. Although he failed the medical for his eyes again, he was accepted 'on appeal', as the senior officer on the Medical Appeals Board said that Patrick had shown the kind of determination that the Royal Navy needed. He passed out from Dartmouth with a first-class pass in his academic studies and with three prizes in different subjects. His reports indicated from early on that he was destined to have a long and successful career.

Patrick did his fleet training on the destroyer HMS *Devonshire* and took part in a sensitive visit to the Soviet Black Sea Fleet in Odessa in the late 1970s. After his next set of exams, in which he achieved another first-class pass, Patrick joined a new frigate while it was being finished – HMS *Ardent*. His next job was in Northern Ireland where, among other duties, he was responsible for finding new refuelling sites for the patrol ships. This meant driving around the Ulster countryside looking at small ports and rivers with an armed Royal Marine as escort. Patrick always carried a personal weapon when ashore on these and other duties. He was fired at by terrorists on at least one occasion, while in a rigid-raider fast boat after he had boarded and searched a small boat. He was part of the Royal Navy's Northern Ireland patrol when IRA terrorists murdered Lord Mountbatten. He had requested the Northern Ireland posting.

In the early 1980s Patrick worked as navigator of HMS *Achilles* which was acting as the West Indies Guard Ship, and then as a principal warfare officer on board frigates HMS *Active* and *Sirius*.

Patrick's next job was one of the most important that he held whilst serving. Throughout the 1970s and 1980s Soviet and NATO submarines routinely ignored international boundaries and chased each other around, occasionally bumping into one another, and sometimes disappearing completely. Since the closest that the Soviet navy had to an Atlantic port is either the northern Russian port of Murmansk, or the ports in one of the Baltic states, any submarine trying to enter the safer and deeper waters of the Atlantic Ocean had somehow to get around Britain. The North Sea on Britain's east coast is too shallow and, when it gets to the English Channel, too narrow to be used safely and secretly, so submarines had to pass between Scotland and the Faeroe Islands, or the Faeroes and Iceland in order to reach the deep ocean proper. The west coast of Scotland was one of the most important locations for anti-submarine warfare throughout the Cold War; as it had been for defending the convoys crossing the North Atlantic from the United States and Canada from wolf packs of Nazi U-boats in the Second World War.

The Royal Navy and the Royal Air Force, with their force of Nimrods (the British version of the P3 Orion, used by the United States and Australia), work together to search out and destroy enemy submarines on Britain's northern flank in time of war. During the 1980s Royal Navy frigates and other NATO warships worked with RAF Nimrods, while shore-based controllers contributed with analysis from other sources of intelligence, to track down Soviet submarines. Patrick Lyster-Todd, now a lieutenant-commander was security cleared to a very high level and worked as the key link between these different units in tracking down submarines.

Later he became the key officer responsible for young officers' training, in Portsmouth. He organised the officer of the watch courses which all young seaman officers complete before taking control of the ship during their watches at sea, and as officer of the day, whilst in port. He made his mark on this job, most notably by encouraging fitness standards for young officers, and improving the system which had previously treated young officers as foolish trainees and not as young professionals. Although some fifteen years older than most of the officers, he always ran the required times and distances for the fitness tests as well.

This job was a significant one designed for a high-flying officer and would almost automatically have resulted in a first lieutenant's job, followed by command of a frigate. He could equally have gone on to command a small ship.

But by this time Patrick's private life had caught up with him. He had always kept his homosexuality completely hidden and was not expecting to be discovered – and ultimately he wasn't – but the existence of the ban caused him to throw in his career for the most unselfish of reasons: to care for his dying partner.

As a secret homosexual with a career ahead of him full of potential, he had never been able to develop an open gay life, visiting gay bars and restaurants with friends and potential lovers. Instead he had taken the route that many secret gay men take – making occasional visits to saunas, where he could meet other men and have sex with them.

There were other elements which gave Patrick cause for worry. His flat in Portsmouth contained videos and magazines that could arouse suspicion, and he made a list of the things he had to move or hide to 'straighten up' his flat before heterosexual colleagues came for dinner or drinks. In 1988 Patrick met Dennis at a sauna in Brighton. He made a rule of not remaining in contact with the men he met at saunas, tearing up the phone numbers when they were exchanged to avoid the temptation. But this time Patrick did stay in touch, and he and Dennis began a relationship. The photographs that Patrick still has of their time together show a very happy couple at home, at play and on holiday. However, Dennis was HIV positive and became ill in 1992.

Patrick wanted to continue his career and did so, but he also wanted to spend time with his lover and care for him. If Dennis had been his wife, then Patrick would have had access to a wide range of welfare agencies and support for servicemen and women and their families. He found himself in a position where he was excluded automatically from these systems which his heterosexual colleagues were able to draw on. He was unable to explain to his colleagues and boss that he had another major call on his time. Caring for somebody with AIDS, even when they have parents as supportive as Dennis's, is heavily demanding on both time and emotion.

Patrick decided that his career was going to have to end. Aware that he was turning down the opportunity of a first lieutenant's job and command at sea – something he had wanted for most of his life – he applied for early retirement.

Dennis's condition became suddenly much worse and he was frequently in and out of hospital. Patrick drove many hundreds of miles a week to and from Dennis's bed but was still at work every day acting as though nothing was happening.

'I got up each morning at seven and was at work by eight. I changed at work and left Portsmouth by six-thirty. I got to the Charing Cross Hospital, in London, by nine pm and left at midnight. I was normally in bed by about two am, and then up to go to work again at seven. Every day.'

The stress was enormous, but Patrick was pleased when his application for early retirement was accepted – the date given for his last day at work was at the beginning of April 1992. Dennis died two days before this date. Lieutenant-Commander Patrick Lyster-Todd retired, honourably, from the Royal Navy after nineteen years of outstanding service, alone.

'I've got salt in my blood. I sometimes stand on the promenade at Southsea and just watch the sea, and two years later it is still depressing, terribly depressing. I knew that I wanted to serve at sea as a seaman and I was damned good at it. The navy has lost me because of this stupid policy. I am glad that I took the decision to leave to look after Dennis, but the fact that he died before I got the time to spend with him will always hurt.'

Two and a half years after his retirement, aged thirty-nine, Patrick is still unemployed. He has applied for hundreds of jobs and reached the interview and second interview shortlist time after time. He has thrown himself behind a wide number of HIV and AIDS initiatives and health promotion schemes in Portsmouth and the wider Wessex Regional Health Authority area. He is a volunteer at the London Lighthouse, the residential and drop-in centre for people with HIV and AIDS. He is looking for work in this area, but the HIV and AIDS care and prevention industry is a difficult one to move into as an 'outsider' – and in what is inevitably a fairly left-wing, 'politically correct' area there is some resentment at the presence of a former member of the armed forces.

The personal motive that led to Patrick's overwhelming desire to work with people who are HIV positive or have an AIDS diagnosis is obvious, but it is his abilities as a manager and motivator that have resulted in his success in voluntary healthcare and prevention. He is looking for work in a narrow field, however, and it will take time to prove that he is qualified to work in these areas.

The loss of Patrick's career, which he still misses enormously, his unemployed status and the waste of the huge sums of money spent training him – all these are due solely to the presence of the ban.

'Of course I still have many friends in the service, and everyone knows now that I'm gay. People are wrong to suggest that it would present a problem for me if I was still in.'

The damage that the ban causes extends beyond those like Steve Purvis and Peter Williams, who are humiliated and sacked. It also goes beyond those who, like Army Lieutenant Elaine Chambers, have to live with the knowledge that their address book and letters have led to a 'witch-hunt' and a number of subsequent dismissals. There are people even further from the minds of those that enforce the current regulations than those who, like Patrick Lyster-Todd, leave because of it, and don't appear in the Government statistics.

Steve, Peter, Elaine and Patrick all have families – mothers, fathers, brothers, sisters – and friends; and the issue of how to break the news to them has to be confronted.

One officer said, 'The interrogation with the SIB was nothing compared with having to tell my parents that I'm gay.'

My experience was the same. I was interviewed at length by SIB investigators in Portsmouth and was then left in limbo. I didn't know what was going to happen – but I was pretty sure that I was going to be discharged, although I was not going to resign voluntarily. I had admitted that I was gay, but was not going to accept that meant I was unable to do my job.

I was not put in touch with any support or welfare agency, despite the fact that many exist for servicemen and women. And I knew nothing of the lesbian and gay groups which exist to help overcome the difficulties of 'coming out' to parents and friends. My mother knew nothing of my homosexuality, and I had done nothing to bring it to her attention.

I had to tell her not only that I had lost my job, but that I was gay and therefore unlikely to get married and produce lots of grandchildren. It was an enormous task – and I didn't make a very good job of it. I started by trying to say that I had just changed my mind about being a Royal Navy officer, and that I was leaving to do other things. Since I didn't have the faintest idea what the 'other things' were, it was not a very convincing argument. It was during the heated discussion about leaving the navy that I had to tell her I was gay and had no choice but to leave. It was not a particularly auspicious 'coming out'.

Some parents are completely unable to deal with the issue, and the relationship between them and their children, who have also been discharged, can be devastated – they lose touch completely. Other parents are more supportive than their children could have anticipated. One navy lieutenant-commander had the following conversation with his Roman Catholic father:

'I'm leaving the navy.'

'Voluntarily?'

'No, I'm not leaving of my own choice.'

'So what is the reason?'

'I'm being dismissed on grounds of homosexuality.'

'Is it true?'

'Yes.'

'Well, you must sue them for unfair dismissal then.'

This is an unusual experience; it takes many parents several months or years to come to terms with what has happened to their son or daughter.

The nature of military culture encourages early marriages and relationships, and since many lesbians and gay men don't actually 'come out' until some years into their careers, a number of them have wives or husbands, and sometimes children as well. They have to break the news to their spouses as well as their parents. Their job, wife, children, relationship with parents, future; all are under threat.

Robbie MacGillivray, a Royal Navy radio operator was twenty when he admitted his homosexuality and was discharged in 1991. He was married with a daughter. During his SIB questioning he told the investigators that he wanted to tell his wife himself, and that he was going to go home to do that. Without his permission the navy visited his wife before he had managed to speak to her. It was not a happy revelation.

By 1994 Robbie MacGillivray had not seen his wife or daughter since he left the navy and despite the fact that he had been unemployed for most of the intervening time, with the odd spell of casual bar-work when he could find it, the Child Support Agency continues to pay very close attention to him. As a result of the navy's visit to his wife, he now has no contact with his daughter.

RAF Sergeant Simon Ingram's partner, David Tolliss, is a young doctor, and by the time Simon was discharged they had been together for a year.

'As a doctor I thought that I really understood how depression would affect Simon when he lost his job. But I really didn't understand – and sometimes I realise that I still don't understand – how much of a part of his life the air force was. If we are in company and there is someone else from a military background there, Simon will talk about air force and military things for hours, while I haven't got the faintest idea what he is talking about. I get very angry when I feel totally excluded from that part of his life. The air force treated him disgracefully and yet he still loves it completely. I know he would go back tomorrow if he could. However hard I try, I cannot really grasp how much a job can grip someone like that. I'm a doctor, which required a huge amount of commitment in training, but I am not obsessed with the lifestyle of being a doctor in the same way that all the people from the forces I've met are obsessed with the military lifestyle.'

The presence of the ban may put more pressure on an individual than he or she can bear. When Flight-Lieutenant

Steve Purvis was court-martialled and found guilty, the information was circulated to other RAF stations – not least because it was in the newspapers. One acquaintance of Steve's who was gay, but not 'out', killed himself a few weeks later.

There were two suicides of servicemen in 1992 and 1993 which can be linked directly to the issue of sexuality. Since the subject was not raised at the inquests, I am not going to add to the grief of the families by giving currency to any rumours that they may have heard. But the Ministry of Defence knows that lesbian and gay servicemen and women have killed themselves rather than face exposure. In view of the pressure put on men and women under suspicion, this is far from surprising. The only way to limit the damage to homosexuals in the services whilst the ban is in place is to ensure that, after exposure, they are given access to proper welfare and support. After all, the mechanisms and departments already exist.

4

IN SUPPORT OF THE STATUS QUO

IN ORDER TO understand the current situation, and the arguments that support the policy currently banning lesbians and gays from serving, we need to understand the nature of service life. After all, supporters of the ban do not argue that homosexuality should be recriminalised in civilian life; at least most of them don't – there are those in the military and in the public at large who believe homosexuality is so unnatural and abhorrent that it remains open to question whether it should be allowed in Britain at all. Sir Nicholas Fairbairn, a Scottish Conservative MP, believed homosexuality should be viewed as the very worst sort of crime. In an interview during the debate on the lowering of the age of consent for male homosexuals in Britain in 1994 he asked if the House of Commons was next going to be asked to consider introducing an age of consent for armed robbery.

It would be unfair to characterise the Ministry of Defence's position as similar to these extremist views. Most liberal-minded people on both sides of the debate would probably want to distance themselves from Sir Nicholas on this issue, and on many others. However, it would also be wrong to suggest that his views are not echoed by many in the armed forces. What is it about military society that gives it a different outlook to much of society at large? Or is there, as the ban's supporters argue, a genuine need to outlaw homosexuality because of the nature of service life? Do the services really *need* to discriminate?

The armed forces have always been considered the ultimate

67

boys' club, the apogee of all that is male and macho. The army and navy traditionally tried to recruit boys as young as they possibly could: boy soldiers and boy seamen fought in both world wars, and it was possible to join the navy at fourteen until surprisingly recently. The army still recruits boys: in Scotland it is possible to join as a soldier at the age of fifteen years and eight months, in England and Wales fifteen years and ten months. The Royal Navy, because of the technical nature of most of its work, now looks for older recruits, many with A levels, and so seventeen is unusually young for most navy recruits. The RAF, formed by combining the army's Royal Flying Corps and the Royal Navy Air Service after the First World War, has always been a slightly older service, although most of the Spitfire and Hurricane pilots who lost their lives during the Battle of Britain were in their late teens or early twenties. Douglas Bader, the outstanding leader of the Duxford Wing during the Battle of Britain in 1940, was one of the most senior and respected flying members of the RAF and he was thirty years old.

For members of the armed forces, life has traditionally revolved around the Mess. This building, or room, or series of rooms, is the real subdivision of personnel that matters in the military system. Platoons, ships' companies, or squadrons are important, but it is life in the Mess – the Officers' Mess, Sergeants' Mess, or Stokers' Mess, that really counts. The Mess is the centre of social life; it may not be a fighting unit, but it is where people live, eat, drink, play and talk. On an air base or army camp, the Mess is effectively the only building or place not directly associated with work. For some junior ranks the NAAFI (Navy, Army, and Air Force Institutes), an 'independent' supplier of services including shops and bars, may be the Mess, but wherever it is, the Mess represents the social relationships between individuals in the forces.

The Mess is a male club. For officers in comfortable establishments it even looks like one: a comfortable bar, a plush reading room, wood-panelled dining room with polished silver trophies, and maybe a squash court or some tennis courts across the gardens. It is generally the only cabin on board a warship with chintzy furnishings (excluding the captain's cabin). A signed portrait of the Queen and Prince Philip will probably hang on a wall or bulkhead somewhere. The dress code is formal for dinner every evening, and the regular Mess dinners are very formal gatherings where speeches are made and the port and madeira are passed strictly to the left. Of course there are now women in the Mess as well – but where they are part of the same Mess they have had to enter on the same terms as the men, effectively becoming honorary men. The Messes which have in essence changed their character to accommodate women are relatively few, and for the most part, women have adopted the customs and rituals that men have built up over the years. From time to time, most Messes have a ladies' night, when women (generally wives and girlfriends) are allowed to dine in as guests. And despite the fact that women are now members of the Messes and can invite boyfriends and husbands, these evenings are still universally known as ladies' nights. The politically correct concept of partners' nights is still a long way off.

Young men and women joining the armed forces are very soon introduced to the rituals that separate service life from civilian drudgery. They are often drawn to the armed forces by the promise of a special way of life. Television and newspaper advertising for a service career emphasises the thrills and adventure available to members of the club: one television advertisement for the army in 1994 showed 'Frank' skiing, running around in combat camouflage gear, jumping out of an aeroplane, and sitting in a forest somewhere with his mates after the war or exercise was over. The message declares unambiguously that this is not civilian life.

From the moment that groups of nervous recruits meet at railway stations in obscure parts of Britain and climb on to coaches bound for their basic training establishment, 'fitting in' is everything. No shell suits and earrings today. All those arguments during adolescence – 'I can wear what I like, Mum' – disappear as young men and women try to conform to a different peer group. Hollywood feature films about the military, *An Officer and a Gentleman*, and *Private Benjamin*, will have prepared these young people for the rigours of basic training – and most will have had a haircut already. As they climb off the coaches and assemble on parade grounds in their civilian clothes, clutching multi-coloured sports bags and suitcases, they are civilians for the last time. Within a week they'll be in uniform, with matching luggage (kit bag and holdall) and marching (albeit badly) in squads around the establishment, saluting everything that moves.

When they pass out of their basic training some weeks or months later, it will be with a great sense of accomplishment. After all, much of the point of basic training is to push recruits hard, harder than they will have been pushed in their civilian lives, and to see how they react. Authority will have been at its most extreme, with lots of pointless rushing around and responding to orders in the hope that responsive young soldiers, sailors and airman will leave their basic training ready to learn their trades or specialisations at other establishments.

Regular inspections on the parade ground ensure that all the recruits are identical, right down to the positioning of the creases on their blouses. Night-time exercises around Aldershot or on Dartmoor or Salisbury Plain exhaust the young men and women who, just when they think it's all over, will be asked to march another six miles, or ford another icy stream.

By the time that their parents, boyfriends, girlfriends and siblings come to see them pass out at a grand parade attended by a senior officer or VIP, they will think of themselves as fully fledged members of the armed forces. Awards will be given for the best academic performance during training, and for the best all-round 'good egg'. The platoon, class or company with the best record will be congratulated on their performance – there is after all no attempt at politically correct mixed-ability comprehensive military education. *Competition is everything*.

Besides competitiveness, uniformity, strength, dogged determination and deference to authority, another quality is required in men – and is expected to be accepted or encouraged by women – and that is regular, ribald and detailed discussions about the sexual desirability of women. A woman who can't at least play along with the game is a lesbian, and a man who can't keep up with the conversation is either a virgin cherry, or a poof, or both.

Several of the gay servicemen I spoke to talked about their trips to 'girlie' sex shows in foreign climes: as a young Royal Navy officer I visited sex shows in St John's, Newfoundland and Montreal. It was the norm. To have said 'no' would have been to reject the group ethos, to have failed to bend to peer pressure, consciously not to be *one of the boys*. We all, except the sad and lonely cases, expressed a constant and determined interest in heterosexual sex.

Lesbian or poof is a term of casual abuse on a day-to-day basis. If a male recruit is unable to run far enough fast enough, or march in step, or get over a rope net on an assault course then he is probably a poof. He will need to run faster and farther, march better, or climb the net more quickly in order to prove that he is not a poof. Women fare no better, although, as we have seen earlier, the logic seems to be reversed in their case. In other words, to succeed in running faster and farther, marching well, or leaping over large obstacles in a single bound, is to open up the suspicion that the woman is not feminine, and therefore, by default, a lesbian.

It may seem like an odd sort of way to justify the ban, but much of the support for its retention comes from those who profess to be worried about the difficulties homosexuals would have if they were to serve openly in this military environment. According to these apologists, the ban is there for the *benefit* of homosexuals, to keep them safe from the dangers they would face from their colleagues. Colonel Charles Moorhouse from the army's directorate of personnel at the Ministry of Defence in London, in an interview for this book, explained:

'I have commanded groups of soldiers in a variety of environments and I'm telling you that if they [homosexuals] were to be part of any unit they would have a really difficult time.'

The present policy claims that the presence of homosexuals

would damage morale and discipline. That argument only makes sense if we accept Colonel Moorhouse's argument that their presence would result in the breakdown of 'morale and discipline' as heterosexual colleagues failed to cope with the presence of gay men and women and attacked their 'out' colleagues. It seems as if the military is defending the need for the continuation of the ban by arguing that without it 'good order' could not be maintained.

The phrase 'prejudicial to good order and discipline' is brought out like a sacred relic by all and sundry in support of the ban and never really questioned. When I was interviewing Colonel Moorhouse and civilian colleague Susan Willett from the Ministry's personnel policy department, I asked them to explain what exactly it was about homosexuality that they felt was so prejudicial. I was repeatedly given the impression that they were genuinely concerned that fear of homosexuals among 'straight' servicemen and women would put homosexuals at risk. The argument seems to be, in essence, that the military is homophobic and therefore homosexuals shouldn't serve – for their own good. There is no suggestion that the homophobia is wrong. The officials simply seem to acknowledge its existence, and use it as a reason to prevent lesbians and gay men from serving.

A series of letters between a junior Royal Navy officer studying at Birmingham University and a senior navy medical officer demonstrates precisely the level of anti-gay sentiment that it is currently acceptable to express in the British armed forces.

Surgeon Commander Richard Jolly OBE, writing in his position as principal medical officer at Britannia Royal Naval College sent a letter to all the naval men and women studying at civilian universities in 1992. The letter contained warnings and enjoinders about the perils of certain aspects of civilian life, and included his views on homosexuality.

> Some of the things that are acceptable and tolerated in civilian life have no place in the disciplined and hierarchical structure of the Armed Services. Homosexuality, for instance, may be legal 'outside', but it has a corrosive effect on the cohesion and

fighting efficiency of a warship. You must understand that although this biologically unsound activity may have recently been decriminalised in military law, it remains illegal in the Service.

A serving heterosexual young officer, found the reference to homosexuality as 'biologically unsound' offensive, and wrote back to Surgeon Commander Jolly expressing his views on the letter:

As it stands, your four lines on homosexuality serve only in showing that homophobia exists at all levels and in all departments within the Royal Navy – a fact about which we should be ashamed. The fact that being gay *is* illegal in the Service does not legitimise the use of offensive remarks which are so blatantly homophobic and especially when they serve no real purpose.

The automatic result of a letter like this, expressing a positive and non-traditional stance on homosexuality, was a visit from the young officer's university liaison officer to talk to him about the inappropriateness of writing such letters, and, more importantly, to make sure that the young officer wasn't gay himself. A month after his original letter of complaint, he received a reply from Surgeon Commander Jolly:

The phrase *biologically unsound* was most carefully chosen. Many of the alternative descriptions of homosexuality that are in current usage in the Fleet might well give offence, even to those who are not apologists for that particular lifestyle. If such a simple (but entirely accurate) labelling caused you to be 'deeply offended', then stand by to become *really* upset. Here are some of the common terms that I could have used:

Brown-hatter	Bowel-troweller
Shirtlifter	Botty bandit
Porthole-gazer	Arse grabber
Uphill gardener	Raving nosh
Beef bosun	Turd burglar

Frankly if you think that you will be able to emulate Don Quixote's approach in stamping out such descriptions of homosexuality in the Royal Navy, then you are very much mistaken. Instead you would be well advised to . . . try never to confuse your duties as a Naval officer with your feelings as a private citizen. Should you ever do so again, then you will be standing into shoal waters and in serious damage of running aground.

Also, think hard about this. While homosexuality makes no real sense from a reproductive, evolutionary or even behavioural standpoint, the bacteriological argument is irrefutable. In design, layout, and function, 'genito-urinary' must always be kept separate from 'gastro-intestinal'. While I very much hope that you will go on to obtain the equivalent of a Double First in your chosen subjects of Sociology and Politics, I know that even if you succeed, you'll still not be able to convince me about the merits of a way of life in which the main sewer gets regular usage as a playground.

These views, which are not rare, present a serious problem for lesbians and gay men wanting to serve. There is no doubt that there is a level of fear about the presence of homosexuals, as there used to be, and in many places still is, about the service of women, particularly at sea. But while the Ministry of Defence has sought actively to argue for women to be accepted, it has made no attempt to break down the prejudice against homosexuality. If Surgeon Commander Jolly's letter had been offensive about women, it would have expressed the general sentiments of the Fleet of only a few years ago, but education, experience, and practice have begun to achieve changes in entrenched sexist attitudes.

The Ministry of Defence's and armed forces' position on issues of social change and development is one of denial: they like to pretend that nothing has changed. In 1993, writing for the *Independent*, I was leaked a copy of some highly classified minutes from a senior management meeting of commanding officers from major warships and flag officers at which the subjects of homosexuality and women at sea were discussed. The commanding officer of HMS *Invincible*, one of Britain's small aircraft carriers, which has a large complement of women, was on record as asking when senior management were going to acknowledge the serious problems which they were experiencing with the integration of women on board.

In preparing the story I approached the Ministry of

Defence for its comments on *Invincible*'s worries. The MOD replied, 'The Ministry of Defence considers the integration of women at sea to be a complete success.' I pointed out that this was evidently not the case, and asked for a serious answer. None came, and the Ministry's head remained firmly stuck in the sand. It became clear that it wasn't just the media who were being stonewalled in such cases. The commanding officer's complaint revealed a deep frustration with an administrative and executive hierarchy which was unprepared to acknowledge social problems and act positively to resolve them.

It was at the time that the Ministry of Defence was failing to grasp the difficulties that the advent of women's service at sea had caused – and thereby take the positive, public, action that is needed to show leadership on issues of this importance – that the new 'Armed Forces Policy and Guidelines on Homosexuality' were being introduced and published in the spring of 1994.

Prior to the issue of these guidelines, which cover all the services, the Ministry of Defence claim that only the Royal Navy had specific written guidelines for dealing with homosexuality. The navy's 'Confidential' guidelines were leaked to the lesbian and gay political lobbying group Stonewall in 1993, which passed them on to the media. These guidelines, in use until at least 1992, treated homosexuality, transvestism, sadism and masochism and 'other forms of sexual deviancy' as a group. The guidelines explained to officers and medical officers what they should do in the event that a man or woman was found, or believed to be, homosexual. The guidelines are no longer in use, but until 1992 people dealing with homosexuals needed to be told, for example that, 'A homosexual act of itself is not life-threatening', and 'homosexuals are often a source of sexually transmitted diseases . . . Tears and stains, in particular of the underpants, trousers and shirt, should be examined and, if available, an ultra-violet light should be used to screen the clothing, bearing in mind that semen is not the only substance which fluoresces under UV light.'

Gin and tonic fluoresces too, so it is a good thing that they pointed it out. The 1994 guidelines do show a much more enlightened understanding of the issues involved, but curiously they fail to give details of the procedures used to investigate possible or suspected homosexuals.

Susan Willett at the Ministry of Defence admitted that the 1987 guidelines were out of date and faintly absurd. She would have been hard-pressed had she not done so when they contained sections like this:

'For evidence whether the man may have played the passive role: a. Note the general appearance. Look for feminine gestures, nature of clothing and use of cosmetics etc.'

Both Ministry of Defence spokespeople said that the other services had not used specific guidelines on the issue before 1994, but had simply enforced Section 64 (Disgraceful Conduct by Officers), Section 66 (Disgraceful Conduct of an Indecent Kind), and Section 69 (Conduct Prejudicial to Good Order and Service Discipline) of the Army Act 1955 and Air Force Act 1955, and Sections 36, 37 and 39 of the Naval Discipline Act 1957 (for the Royal Marines).

Speaking of the new policy, Susan Willett said: 'We are quite happy with our new policy. We had good reason to alter the old, not least because the Armed Forces Bill Select Committee had made recommendations which the Ministry of Defence accepted and these needed to be spelled out.'

When Colonel Moorhouse was asked why our NATO colleagues seem not to need a similar ban he explained: 'The nature of our services is different from the countries that you mention. We have a worldwide commitment and our men and women live much more closely together for extended periods of time.'

I pointed out that gay Dutch soldiers were currently serving in Rwanda and Bosnia. Colonel Moorhouse responded: 'I have lived and worked with a Dutch battalion. Their attitude and style is completely different. They have trade unions, and wear their hair down their back and only seem to work a two-day week. There is no comparison. Also they have a political agenda which is absent here, it is a different political situation.'

Both of the spokespeople dealt with the issue of discrimination in the workplace. I suggested that the armed forces try to present themselves as equal opportunity employers, but are in reality far from that. Susan Willett explained that the armed forces were discriminatory, and had to be.

'It is only the pregnant women case that has made the Sex Discrimination Act apply to us, and we had to defend that in court. We have to discriminate about what people can and can't do. The colour of someone's skin does not matter, but their gender and sexuality do. It is ridiculous for you to equate sexuality with skin colour. It's not the same and we have to have some kind of control. The close confines in which people are living, the rank structure and the general problem of military conditions give maximum opportunity for homosexuals to cause problems.'

Colonel Moorhouse took up the theme: 'The services view sexuality very distantly. It is not an area that the services really deal with at all, sexuality of any sort is not dealt with. The conditions in which the military serve are not conducive to allowing homosexuals to serve. The military is about control – the ethos is one of control, and emotions are not easy to control. The ships which have women on board operate a "no touch" rule, it's like prep school – there's an Islamic-style "purdah" in operation in these close-quarters environments. We don't need the additional pressure.'

Several times during my interview the Ministry of Defence spokespeople came back to their central point which seems to be that the other servicemen and women, the 'straight' men and women, would find homosexuality difficult.

'The instinctive reaction is difficult – this is not a forty-hour-week job and people have to live together. Men and women on board ships have separate showering arrangements – but within each sex they share the same facilities.'

Colonel Moorhouse nodded when I asked if he felt that all-gay units would be able to function. The root of the reason for the ban seems to be the nature of the relationships between the heterosexual and homosexual members of the armed forces, rather than something intrinsic to the nature of homosexuality itself.

In the United States the situation is the same: US policy explains in detail the process that should take place after discovery of homosexuality, the dry policy position, but nowhere does it explain precisely what it is in the nature of homosexuality that makes it 'incompatible with military service'.

Colonel Moorhouse used the phrase in many different ways. 'The idea of homosexuality in the military workplace is incompatible. Our job is to defend the country, and that needs a teamed disciplined fighting machine – we can't have all the job areas open to just anyone.'

Still no explanation of precisely what it is about homosexuality that makes it 'incompatible' – so much more 'incompatible' than misogyny, racism, heterosexual harassment, and child abuse that it needs to be specifically outlawed.

The British army recently asked a court to deal leniently in its sentencing of a soldier found guilty of sexual offences against a child, as they said he was a valued soldier and they did not want to dismiss him. *Fortunately for him*, the victim was a girl.

The discharges continue, and I asked the spokespeople to explain why it took so many months to deal with them. They expressed surprise and were clearly under the impression that they were effected speedily and with care.

I cited the case of RAF Corporal Ian Waterhouse who had been kept at work for seven months and expected to carry weapons with live ammunition. Susan Willett said, 'I have no answer for that. I had envisaged he would be out within a month.'

The MOD officials are clearly out of touch with much of the reality of their policy in action. They did not believe that service policemen routinely carry out surveillance on lesbian and gay establishments in their areas, although they did admit that they could believe that surveillance would be carried out on an individual after information, including anonymous letters, had been received. One of the officials said, 'Policemen are very difficult to control, they have their regulations and they follow them. You can't tell them what to do. It is not possible to disconnect the police from this matter, particularly in the Royal Navy and RAF, where so much security clearance is involved, even at a junior level. If you tell me that this kind of surveillance is taking place then it's beyond the call of duty. Policemen have got to have their own agenda.' (I had always thought of 'beyond the call of duty' as a commendation.)

Clearly, since it has little idea of the time and energy expended investigating homosexuality, it is not at all surprising that the Ministry of Defence is unable to put a cost on the investigations. In an answer to Barbara Roche MP who asked how much these investigations cost, Lord Henley, Parliamentary Under-Secretary of State for Defence, wrote:

> You also ask for the cost of employing investigators in each Service to investigate allegations of homosexuality. The Service's investigating units are employed to investigate all alleged breaches of Service discipline or law and the investigation of allegations of homosexuality is just one of their tasks. There are no separate units specifically designed to investigate such allegations and, therefore, no separate costs are required to be held.

Lord Henley's response in the same letter to Barbara Roche's questions about costs of dismissal is in the same tone: 'You ask what records are kept to indicate how long it took those dismissed to find work, how long they were dependent on State benefits and at what cost to the tax-payer. We hold no such records and to obtain the information would entail disproportionate effort.'

I asked the spokespeople how the armed forces managed to work alongside civilian contractors, senior civil servants and members of other armed forces who were legally 'out' lesbians or gay men.

Colonel Moorhouse explained: 'We work alongside gays in civilian life all the time, of course we do. The difference is in the control of the individual that we require. I suppose that if you behave discreetly in the British Armed Forces there would not necessarily be a problem. But once your sexuality is known then the issue of control becomes important and discharge is appropriate.'

The spokespeople explained the situations in which men or women found to have engaged in homosexual activity are not dismissed: 'There can be cases of retention when you're talking about an isolated incident with a young person, or if the allegations cannot be substantiated – a warning would be appropriate in these circumstances. But provided the commanding officer is satisfied that the individual is gay, then they will be discharged.'

Spokespeople for the Labour Party and the Liberal Democrats have both made statements in the past about the foolishness of the current policy. I asked the Ministry of Defence spokespeople how they would react if in 1996 they were required to change the policy in the event of a Labour Party General Election victory. Would the defence of Britain fall apart?

'If we are forced to change the policy then of course we will – we do not make policy, that is a matter for Government. The Services would have to look at the new realities and try to overcome the problems,' said Susan Willett.

Colonel Moorhouse outlined the problems he would foresee more specifically: 'There would be very real problems. Parents would be concerned about allowing their young people to join. Presently serving individuals would leave in reaction, and there would be problems when individuals refused to share housing. All sorts of problems about married quarters would follow. It's like the problem of men wanting paternity leave. You might as well say do you see us allowing drugs in the Service. It's not going to happen, or if it does it is so far away that we won't be here to write the new policy.'

Both officials seemed unconcerned about the possibility of European Court action, and carefully pointed out that a European Court of Human Rights ruling would not automatically be binding on them.

One issue raised by many of the individuals I met during my research was the lack of health and 'safe-sex' advice available to serving homosexuals. It was explained to me that the

Health Education Authority leaflet has been used and distributed amongst members of the armed forces, but that it had been over-printed with the information that contact with some of the organisations listed on the leaflet, including the Terrence Higgins Trust, could be considered 'incompatible'.

When units or individuals visit Africa in particular they are warned about the dangers of HIV infection. There is no mention of homosexuality.

At the conclusion of this very frank and helpful interview, I asked for an authoritative statement of the current policy from the Government. It took a letter from a former Foreign Office Minister, Tristan Garel-Jones, to persuade the Secretary of State, Malcolm Rifkind, to outline the definitive Government position at the time of writing. The Secretary of State wrote:

> The Ministry of Defence has long taken the view that the special conditions of Service life preclude the acceptance of homosexuals and homosexual activity. It acknowledges the requirement for Service personnel to live in close proximity with others in single-sex accommodation, to work at times under great stress and in close quarters with their colleagues, and with complete trust and confidence between all ranks. Such a requirement is quite different from civilian life and the potentially disruptive influence of homosexual relationships and practices has to be excluded. In particular it is essential that there should be no possibility that the authority of senior rank should be exploited for sexual ends, or that junior members of the Services should be coerced into acts in which they would not choose to engage in normal circumstances. Furthermore, there is also the possibility that any members of the Forces engaging in homosexual acts might be vulnerable to blackmail and therefore present a security risk: not all those who are of homosexual orientation or engage in homosexual activities are prepared to admit it as they may fear the reactions from their family and friends.

5

SECURITY RISK

SINCE THE FIRST World War every member of the armed forces, as well as men and women in Government and the intelligence services, has had to have security clearance in order to have access to sensitive information. As a result security clearance and the process of 'vetting' – investigation of an individual to see if he or she poses a security risk – have been an important part of the process of military advancement; no clearance, no job.

For many years the Ministry of Defence justified the ban on lesbians and gay men on the basis of the potential risk they said that they would pose to security. Certainly, while homosexuality was still outlawed in civilian life the potential for blackmail by enemy agents was real, but is this really still the case?

The publicity surrounding the Cambridge spy ring in the 1950s did an enormous amount of damage to the way in which homosexuality was viewed by the security establishment. As Burgess, Maclean, Philby and Blunt were uncovered as spies the rumours about their sexuality began. Unfortunately this group has been perceived more as a homosexual ring than as an ideological body, despite the fact that they were not all gay. It is true that Guy Burgess in particular lived an almost completely open gay life which was remarkable in the 1930s and 1940s. Everyone who needed to know about his sexuality prior to his defection, knew; and yet nothing was done. The end result of the defections was that the 'Burgess lifestyle' – too much alcohol, too many boys and a predilection for musical theatre have been synonymous in the official mind with treason ever since.

The case of the most notorious victim of KGB blackmail in modern times, a gay Admiralty clerk caught in 1962 who had passed over documents for seven years, shows how entrapment and blackmail worked. William John Vassall was entrapped whilst working at the British embassy in Moscow by a gay Polish clerk, Sigmund Mikhailski, who had been planted there by the Russians. He reported that Vassall seemed a likely candidate for blackmail, and after a series of dinners in Moscow flats Vassall was photographed next to a naked Russian man on a sofa. Shortly afterwards the KGB burst in on him whilst he was with a half-dressed handsome Russian military officer, who had obviously been planted. Blackmail was not the only motive. Vassall accepted large sums of money from the Russians and spent much of it furnishing his flat in Dolphin Square – the establishment apartment buildings next to the River Thames. Vassall's treachery only served to confirm in the official mind the link between homosexuality and breaches of security. The comment was made at the time that it was the illegality of homosexuality itself that posed the risk. Donald Maclachlan, a former naval intelligence officer and first editor of the *Sunday Telegraph*, from 1961 to 1966, said: 'To the Whitehall of 1962 he is in the category that a Jacobite was in 1745 or a Catholic in the days of the Spanish Armada: unreliable because he cannot altogether help it: a potential traitor because he has a guilty secret.'

At the time of the Vassall affair the security service did not routinely keep information on, or ask about, homosexuality. After the embarrassment of this incident, that was rectified. Nowadays, on entry to the armed services, all new recruits are vetted on a basic level – their identity and status will be checked and the security service records consulted. Simply being a member of the armed forces does not confer complete security clearance on any individual.

New recruits also have to sign a copy of part of the Official Secrets Act – which is a strange process. The Act, which defines the crimes that spies commit, applies to everyone in Britain. Signing a copy of the Act does not make the law apply any more or less to the individual who has signed it. It is rather like insisting that all men and women who pass their driving test sign a copy of the Road Traffic Act. No motorist in Britain has signed a copy of the Act, but nevertheless we are all bound by it.

The security machine is extremely complicated and there are a number of different levels of clearance, each level allowing access to documents and places that are 'classified': the operations room on board a ship is one such area.

Each 'classified' item is put into a precise category that defines exactly how secret it is. The categories available are Restricted, Confidential, Secret, and Top Secret – and the category is chosen by deciding how damaging to the nation disclosure of the information would be. For an item to be classified Top Secret the armed forces would have to judge that its disclosure would cause 'exceptionally grave damage to the nation'.

As members of the armed forces reach a level where they need access to documents and information graded above Secret they go through a process known as positive vetting. This is the same process which members of the civilian intelligence agencies, senior civil servants and political advisers have to go through. It is often thought that the security service, MI5, is responsible for vetting and security decisions, but in fact it has long been a matter of Government policy that security and clearance decisions should be made by the individual departments themselves. MI5, however, is often closely involved in the vetting process, particularly if an individual is going to be 'indoctrinated', and given access to material with a Top Secret classification made even more restricted by the addition of codewords describing more precise areas of information. Information about our independent nuclear deterrent is one such area, protected by Top Secret codeword classification. The protective security branch of MI5, which also advises on action to counter threats to national security from other sources including terrorism, offers advice to the Ministry of Defence on these individual clearance decisions, but it does not make the decisions itself. If MI5 had information about the sexuality of an individual which it felt relevant to the vetting process, it would probably pass that information on to the security department of the appropriate service, but it is the individual Army, Royal Navy, or Royal Air Force security department which is responsible for decision-making. The responsibility for the control of information in MI5's vetting advice rests with the Home Secretary and not the Secretary of State for Defence.

Positive vetting, or being 'PV'ed, can be a terrifying process for a lesbian or a gay serviceman because they know that their personal lives will be investigated. Family, wives and co-habitees are all interviewed to ensure there are no subversive skeletons in closets. At least two interviews, one with a close family member, and one with a friend or colleague as referee, are carried out in order to ensure that the serviceman or woman is not, among other things, a communist or homosexual.

Robbie MacGillivray, a gay Royal Navy radio operator, was nineteen when he was positively vetted. A high level of security clearance is required to be a member of the department on board ship which processes and decodes all the incoming classified signals. Robbie's mother and a close friend, also in the Royal Navy, were interviewed and must have given satisfactory answers since he was given the clearance he needed. During Robbie's own vetting interview he was asked if he was, or if he knew anybody who was, homosexual. He said no, although in reality he was still unsure, and had already begun to have sexual experiences with other men.

It is important to be clear about what a member of the armed forces faces when undergoing the positive vetting process. It is a striking example of the kind of dilemma lesbians and gays face throughout their military careers. To lie unambiguously at an interview intended to verify your suitability for access to classified material is a serious offence – and not something which many committed members of the armed forces want to do; to answer the question honestly, however, would result in an immediate investigation and automatic dismissal.

In Britain and the United States those who oppose dropping the ban have claimed for many years that there are 'security reasons' for its continuation, and that individuals who practise a homosexual lifestyle, such as Vassall, are inherently prone to blackmail. For many years this was undoubtedly true – homosexual behaviour was a criminal offence which would result in the complete disgrace and ostracism of the individual involved. But in these more enlightened times most reasonable men or women would not seriously suggest that Sir Ian McKellen or American Congressman Gerry Studds should be locked up for adult consensual homosexual activity.

In fact it is only the existence of the ban itself which provides grounds for blackmail. The only real threat which a potential blackmailer can hold over a member of the armed forces whom they know to be gay, is that they will disclose to the Ministry of Defence their knowledge of the individual's sexuality.

In the United States the security issue was examined by the navy first in 1957 through an officially appointed Board of Inquiry. The report, known as the Crittenden Report, was submitted in March 1957. Although security matters were not a key part of its area of study, it made a number of findings in the area: 'The Board was unable to uncover any statistical data to prove or disprove that homosexuals are in fact more of a security risk than those engaged in other unsocial or immoral conduct.'

And: 'The number of cases of blackmail as a result of past investigations of homosexuals is negligible. No factual data exist to support the contention that homosexuals are a greater risk than heterosexuals.'

The report went on to state, 'Isolated cases are mentioned, but to determine that a homosexual is more of a security risk than a non-homosexual, these instances would have to be measured against security breaks by non-homosexuals, and against the proper observation of security by homosexuals.'

The overall conclusion was that there seems to be nothing inherent in homosexuality which makes homosexuals more likely to present a security threat than anybody else:

There is considerable information which would indicate that other factors in the personality constitute the security risk rather than the factor of homosexuality alone. One such item, for example, would be feelings of inadequacy which drive a man to boast of the secrets he possesses. Such boasting might very well be done to any sexual partner, whether the partner be homosexual or heterosexual. Some intelligence officers consider a senior officer having illicit heterosexual relations with the wife of a junior officer or enlisted man is much more of a security risk than the ordinary homosexual.

The 1957 Crittenden Report also stated explicitly that there were many documented instances of individuals who had been identified as homosexual but who had gone on to serve honourably and well.

The US Navy refused to release this report for more than twenty years: it finally took a court order to force the Defense Department to release it. The British Ministry of Defence states that it has never undertaken any study of homosexuality, or of homosexuality and its possible connection to security violations.

More recently, in 1986, the US Defense Department set up the Defense Personnel Security Research and Education Center (PERSEREC) in Monterey, California. The unit was created in the wake of a series of spy scandals in the mid-1980s and was tasked with two main functions: to perform personnel security research and analysis, and to furnish instruction and advice on personnel security research to other parts of the Defense Department. It operates under control from the Defense Department in Washington DC, and reports to the Assistant Secretary of Defense. One of its first research tasks was to examine and clarify relationships between risk and various personal characteristics, including sexual orientation.

The researchers who wrote the final report took their brief further than the Defense Department had intended they should, and examined the question of whether homosexuals are 'suitable' for military service. Their report, entitled *Nonconforming Sexual Orientations and Military Service*, examines the issues in great detail and looks at a range of literature relating to lesbians and gay men, recent medical and social papers and theses, and litigation relating to the issue. The report finds that lesbians and gay men pose no particular security risk, and also that there are no reasons why lesbians and gays should not serve.

The arrival of the completed report at the Pentagon put the proverbial cat amongst the pigeons. In a letter from the Under-Secretary for Defense, the Defense Department expressed its horror at a report which had: 'Missed the target. Moreover, you exceeded your authority by extending the research effort beyond the personnel security arena, and into another area entirely, namely suitability for military service.'

And another internal Defense Department memorandum stated what perhaps was the real concern:

> It most probably will cause us in Washington to expend even more time and effort satisfying concerns in this whole issue both in Congress and the media, and within the Department itself . . . If it were not for all of the above, the situation could be humorous. It is as if Consumers' Reports commissioned research on the handling characteristics of the Suzuki Samurai, and received instead a report arguing that informal import quotas for Japanese automobiles were not justified.

The report was changed and the authors chastised, but there were considerable concerns about the security of the original report: 'We have invoked the tightest controls on the reproduction of and access to all copies. Except for the three copies sent to Mr Pollari for security review, all our copies are accounted for and kept under secure storage.'

'Out' gay Congressman Gerry Studds managed after a long battle to get hold of a copy of the report. He wrote later: 'During five months of calling, writing, and cajoling, my office was told variously that the report was "unavailable", "still under consideration", that it would be "released soon", and on occasion even that "no such report exists". This stonewalling only served to underscore to me the document's importance.'

No study of homosexuality and security in the armed forces in the last forty years in Britain or the United States has shown that lesbians and gay men pose more of a risk than heterosexuals. The only possible exception to this is an odd document written by a highly decorated US Marine colonel, Ronald D. Ray, published in 1992. Colonel Ray's thesis is that homosexuality in all its forms is dangerous and un-natural and utterly incompatible with military service. He describes in full anatomical detail precisely what he believes constitutes homosexual sexual activity, and goes on to ex-plain why lesbians and gay men present a threat to security:

> Several homosexual apologists and even 60 Minutes' Mike Wallace have all claimed that 'no evidence' exists that homo-sexuals present as a security risk. The Chairman of the House Intelligence Committee and others encouraged the Director of the CIA to stop the long-standing practice of asking potential CIA employees whether they are homosexual in lie detector tests and also stopped investigating sexual preference when updating security clearances.
>
> *The decision followed a 1991 study, ordered by Mr Gates and encouraged by Mr McCurdy, that found no case of a CIA employee's ever having been blackmailed into committing espionage on account of homosexuality.*
>
> Yet Americans, including some in the CIA, have been 'turned' after blackmail threats related to homosexual be-haviour. James Speyer Kronthal had been entrapped by photographs of his sexual activity twice by hostile intelligence services; first by the Gestapo before World War II, and later by the KGB, while he was serving as the CIA Station Chief in Bern, Switzerland. A protegé of Allen Dulles, Kronthal, after being threatened with exposure, provided information to the Soviets for six years before apparently committing suicide in 1953, not long after Dulles offered him a high intelligence position when Dulles became Director of Central Intelligence.

After quoting this pre-war example, Colonel Ray sticks with his historic theme and goes on to cite the Bloomsbury set, the social and literary group in London during the 1930s, in support of his thesis that homosexuality is by its nature a risk to security. He writes: 'The key to understanding modernity and Bloomsbury is sodomy.'

Colonel Ray expounds at length about Bloomsbury and the harm that it has done to the moral fibre of the West: 'Along with their homosexuality they developed an amoral, irreligious attitude and unpatriotic as well [sic]. E. M. Forster, a member of the Bloomsbury [set], was quoted as saying, "If I had to choose between betraying my country and betraying my friend, I hope I should have the guts to betray my country."'

Colonel Ray believes that homosexuality poses a threat to security because of its very nature as a disturbed condition. He pre-empts possible counter-arguments based on American medical and psychiatric opinion by explaining that these professional bodies have been taken over by homosexual activists against their better professional judgement. Perhaps the American medical and psychiatric professional bodies have both been over-run with 'homosexualists', but it seems unlikely that the British Medical Association, the British Royal College of Psychiatrists and a wealth of European equivalent bodies, as well as the United Nations, have all had their policies on sexuality successfully hijacked by a revolutionary lesbian and gay agenda.

Colonel Ray examines the biblical aspects of the ban. It is not my intention to ridicule the arguments that lesbians and gay men pose a very real security risk by quoting foolish examples, but this is the only published argument to support the idea and its pseudo-Christian homophobic inspiration is clear throughout.

Another American report, from the Defense Department in 1989, which was commissioned to look at the 'implications for security clearance suitability' of homosexuals, concluded: 'Homosexuals show pre-service suitability adjustment that is as good or better than the average heterosexual. Thus, these results seem to be in conflict with conceptions of homosexuals as unstable, maladjusted persons. Given the critical importance of appropriate policy in the national security area, additional research attention to this area is warranted.'

Rather than concentrate on what Colonel Ray has to say, perhaps it would be more productive to examine the cases of individuals in the armed forces who have served in sensitive positions whilst they knew they were lesbian or gay.

RAF Sergeant Graeme Grady lived and worked in Washington DC at the British embassy with his wife and children until May 1994. He was the chief clerk to the British Defence Intelligence Liaison Staff and provided the key link between the British and American defence intelligence agencies.

'I joined the Royal Air Force in 1980 and trained as a clerk. I was not gay then, at least I didn't identify as gay, I was aware of feelings I had about men, but I suppressed them. It wasn't acceptable to be gay. I suppose when I really think back I can remember finding a girlfriend's brother very attractive while I was in junior school, but I denied these feelings, and I suppose that's why in some ways I was always the loner. I joined the RAF on 12 August – the same date that thirteen years later I signed the statement admitting to being homosexual.'

At thirty-one Graeme Grady is a striking dark-haired man with a soft East Midlands accent. He was brought up in Leicester and had very little homosexual experience: 'When I was sixteen I played strip-poker with a friend and as we lost our clothes one thing led to another and we ended up getting together. But that was a one-off. After I joined I met a gorgeous guy when I was eighteen who wanted to write to me, but I didn't keep in touch because I knew it would be dangerous. I conformed instead and had girlfriends. I've had sexual relationships with three women – and one of them was my wife, of course. She was more experienced than me when we got married and we had a really good relationship. We got married in 1987, although part of me knew that I shouldn't be doing it. I had not begun to think of myself as gay. I certainly do not regret getting married – we have two children and I will never regret that – it was the right thing to do.'

He served at RAF bases all over Britain, and in the Falkland Islands during the 1980s, becoming a personnel clerk in 1983.

In 1985 he was promoted to corporal and in 1988 became an instructor at the RAF's administration school at Hereford. In 1990 he was promoted to sergeant and then in 1991, after extensive vetting, he was posted to Washington DC to work with the intelligence staff.

'It wasn't really a case of lying in the vetting interviews, I did not think that I was gay. Some colleagues were interviewed as well – but no one thought I was gay then anyway. I was cleared to an extremely high level and went on to my new job. I really cannot say much about the work at all – except that we liaised between the British and American defence intelligence agencies and had representatives of both nations in our building. We arranged visits to and from the British agencies, and had all material passed between the two countries going through our office – it was a sensitive post. My boss was a colonel, and I had three other people under me in the office. It was a tri-service office.'

If Graeme had been made a successful blackmail target he would have posed a very serious threat to the working relationship between the various agencies represented in his office. The intelligence relationship between Britain and the United States is vital, but has been damaged in the past by leaks in the system. If Graeme had become one of those leaks, it would have been a very big story. But he wasn't; he carried out his job effectively and well.

'My family lived with me in Virginia and we had a great time. My wife and I had a great relationship, we never really argued about anything and she knows me inside out. But in 1993 as I was approaching thirty I started to have real crises about turning thirty. Life was going on and I knew that I was not totally happy. I knew that something was going to happen. My wife went back for a month during the summer to see grandparents and stuff in England, and I knew that I was going to find out what was going on in my life then. I was going to meet someone – and I did, in a clothes store at the shopping mall at Potomac Mills – he was the manager and had a boyfriend, but I had a wife, and we ended up having an affair. I knew then that I was gay, and that there was no way I could keep it a secret from my wife – she knew me too well anyway. On the Friday when she got back she knew something was wrong immediately and we had a difficult weekend until the Monday when we sat down to talk about it. She said, "There's someone else isn't there?" and when I said yes she asked if it was a man. She wanted us to stay together, and found a group – they have "groups" for everything in the States – for gay married men. It also had a group for the wives, and we started going – although she had to persuade me at first. She was amazed that there were so many people in the same situation. I was nervous about going to the group at first, but it helped a lot.'

However, it was through the 'help' group that Graeme was to find his career crashing down around him. He was recognised by his colonel's nanny, who was a lesbian. She did not really understand the implications of what she was doing when she told the colonel's wife, who told the colonel, who, it seems, was horrified to discover that he had a gay sergeant and a lesbian nanny. He took 'appropriate action' and reported the fact to London.

So, on 16 May 1993, Sergeant Grady was called unexpectedly to the embassy. He was told that there was a problem about his security clearance, and that he was to be flown back to London that evening. Graeme went home and packed a bag for two days and told his wife that he thought he had been found out. That evening he flew from Dulles airport to RAF Brize Norton, where he was met by RAF policemen who escorted him to RAF Uxbridge. The wing commander there explained that he knew there was a question about his security, though not what it was, and Graeme had to stay in the United Kingdom. He was told that he would not be going back to Washington.

It was another ten days before Graeme had his first interview with the RAF police; in the interval his wife and friends in Washington had been interviewed. He was asked if he was gay. He denied it, and eventually asked to see a solicitor.

'On her advice I simply said "No comment" to the questions, and at that point they announced that they were going to search my luggage and the room I was using at the RAF station. My main concern was that I had been separated from my wife and children and had no real means of explaining to them what was happening.

'I spoke to my boss and asked whether someone in my position who was gay would be entitled to the full range of resettlement grants and benefits. I was worried about supporting my children while I looked for another job, and I needed to know that I wouldn't be left without a penny.'

Graeme's boss didn't know what the situation was, but found out, and was able to reassure Graeme that someone 'caught out' would not lose all his resettlement grant.

'Once I knew that I wouldn't be leaving my family without any money I was prepared to go back into the next interview and tell them that I was gay. I was then asked a whole series of questions about who did what to whom – they wanted graphic details about what we did in bed, and I told them. The interview went on for some time. Some time later I was subjected to a "pressure" interview because of my security clearance, which was conducted by two civilians. It wasn't actually very pressured at all, but they wanted to know if I had been with anyone who could have put pressure on me.'

In Washington Graeme was earning about £25,000 a year – when he was finally sacked from the Royal Air Force ten days before Christmas 1994 he received a resettlement grant of about £5,000.

'I did my job well, and my wife knew that I was gay. There was no security threat involved at all. Why have I lost my job?'

Why indeed? Jason, a senior NCO working in intelligence in one of the armed forces, lives a married double life and intends to continue doing so: 'I have decided that if it ever becomes an issue, or if a serious investigation about me starts then I will be open about the fact that I am gay. I'm more worried about my wife than the job. My work is important and I love it. I'm not going to give it up without a bloody good reason. My job is what I joined to do and I do it well. You can't expect me to throw everything in and piss off just because I'm gay. I know, and you know, that I'm perfectly capable of doing what is a difficult and sometimes dangerous job.'

Those lesbians and gay men who have been positively vetted and work in sensitive positions have had to think carefully about what they would do if somebody did try to blackmail them. The fact that homosexuality has become so visible in day-to-day civilian life – on the television and in the newspapers – means that being forced 'out' is not the terrible threat that it once was. However, the loss of your job, particularly if you have a wife and family to support, puts the potential blackmailer in a very strong position.

6

THE BLACKMAILER'S CHARTER

IN 1895 OSCAR Wilde was convicted of offences under the 1885 Criminal Law Amendment Act, which outlawed consenting homosexual acts between men, even if they were committed in private. The particular section which was to have dramatic effects in the years that followed was passed late at night, just before the summer recess, by an almost deserted House of Commons. A judge at the time dubbed the new law 'The Blackmailer's Charter', and Oscar Wilde would himself write of the 'monstrous martyrdoms' that occurred during his lifetime and would continue for the eighty-two years that the law remained on the statute book. However, 'The Blackmailer's Charter' still exists for members of the armed forces.

As we saw in Chapter 5, the security risks posed by lesbians and gay men are caused by the existence of the ban on them serving in the armed forces, and not by something intrinsic in the nature of homosexuality. The Ministry of Defence acknowledges that there will always be some lesbian and gay people serving secretly, and as long as it remains the case that when they are 'outed' they will lose their jobs, then the possibility for blackmail remains.

Blackmail is not just a theoretical possibility: while researching for this book I came across a case in which two successful naval officers serving on destroyers, one of whom could shortly have been working for the Prime Minister, had their careers destroyed by a determined blackmailer. One of them was blackmailed for over a year before the pressure of the situation affected his behaviour so substantially that the affair came to light.

At the time of writing, in October 1994, both officers are still in the navy, awaiting confirmation of their dismissals. The individual who initiated the events that were to lead to them losing their jobs is still working in the City, apparently being courted by the Royal Navy SIB in the hope that he will reveal more information about serving lesbians and gay men. He is also mentally unstable.

Graeme Ross joined the Royal Navy from university in 1988. He had known he was gay from an early age, but had never come out. Six foot one inch tall, fifteen stone, a keen rugby player and a competitive swimmer, Graeme does not look or act like a stereotypical gay man, and none of his friends at university knew that he was gay. He did not visit a gay bar until he was twenty-five.

'I went to my first gay pub in Glasgow in 1991 while I was based up at Faslane. At the end of 1991 I was posted to Northwood, and in February 1992 I started going out in London to visit gay bars. I didn't know where the gay bars were, so I eventually plucked up the courage to phone the Lesbian and Gay Switchboard to find out. I called from a pay-phone as I was so paranoid about things. I found the Brief Encounter bar, which is pretty seedy, and after walking past a few times went in and rushed to the bar, bought a drink, and then hid in the corner. After a few visits I found out about other nicer places and met a few people. There were probably four or five people that I met more than once, because I was worried about being known. I couldn't risk a long-term re-lationship.'

In October 1992 Graeme, a lieutenant in the supply branch, was appointed to HMS *Manchester*, a modern destroyer, which was coming out of refit in Plymouth.

'As we were still in dock we had lots of free time and I spent weekends in London and Cardiff. We came out of refit and the ship went back to Portsmouth, but I still kept going up to London, meeting people, but I found that in bars you never meet the right sort of person. On my Easter leave in 1993 I was standing in Brief Encounter playing the fruit machine when a guy came up and started speaking to me. He asked me back to his flat, and although I didn't really fancy him I said yes and went back with him to Waterloo. I had no intention of seeing him again, but in the morning he gave me a lift to the station and had breakfast with me saying how much he wanted to see me again.'

The man whom Graeme and others were going to regret meeting was David Varney. He had guessed that Graeme was in the forces, but thought he was in the army. Graeme let him continue thinking that he was an army officer, because he was concerned about his personal security.

David Varney said that he was going to New York for a holiday the following week, and why didn't Graeme go too. Graeme left saying no, but later he changed his mind, and phoned David to say yes.

'It was a spur of the moment decision as I had no real plans for Easter leave and had always wanted to go to America. It was the biggest mistake I have ever made. During the trip I made it clear that I wanted to be friends, that was all, and did not want to have a relationship. I made that absolutely clear.'

Graeme kept vaguely in touch with David after their return, but he found that David had another agenda.

'He had taken down my car registration and used a friend in the police to trace the number to me. Then he phoned the Ministry of Defence and managed to get my service details. He found out that I was in the navy, my rank, and where I was serving. He learned which ship I was on. When I next phoned him he said he had been to a fortune teller who had said that "Manchester" was going to figure in his life. Although I was serving on HMS *Manchester* I feigned ignorance and he then told me what he had found out. He said that he wanted to see me every weekend.'

David seems to have spent huge amounts of time on the phone tracking down pieces of information about Graeme, and started ringing him on the ship whenever it was alongside and connected to the switchboard at Portsmouth, or linked up to a temporary number abroad. Graeme never gave him the number, but David always managed to track it down.

'He phoned me when we were alongside in Denmark and France. The fact that a call for me has been received is piped over the whole ship, and I then had to tell him that I couldn't talk to him. He would get really upset and I was very worried about the situation. I had told him specifically never to phone me on board on many occasions.'

On one weekend when the ship was alongside in Portsmouth, Graeme drove up to London for a night out without telling David where he was going. David went from bar to bar looking for him until he succeeded in finding him.

'He started shouting abuse at me in the bar and followed me out when I left. He was shouting and screaming and crying in the street. I had to stop and apologise to him to prevent a scene. I went back to his flat because I was worried about what he might do. I tried to make it clear that I did not want to sleep with him, but he would immediately fly into a temper tantrum and I had to calm him down. I feel disgusted about it now, but I had to keep sleeping with him. Later he would regularly threaten to phone the navy's police if I didn't fulfil his expectations.

'In June 1993 HMS *Manchester* visited Liverpool, and I went from there to Manchester and visited one of the city's gay pubs, where I was seen by one of Varney's friends, who phoned him. When he next phoned me on board I was in front of other people and he started a tirade of abuse, so I had to go ashore late at night and when I called him back he started shouting and giving me further abuse. I managed to calm him down and agreed to see him next time I was in London. It was after this incident that I decided to tell him at our next meeting that I didn't want anything more to do with him.

'The following weekend I went to his flat in London and took my belongings away from there. I told him that I was sick of him constantly phoning me on the ship and harassing me. I told him that I did not want to see him again. The next day he found me again in a bar and stood for about half an hour at the other end of the bar smirking at me. When he eventually came over to speak to me he held a piece of paper with the name of a master at arms and regulating petty officer [Royal Navy policemen] and some Portsmouth phone numbers on it. He said, "I think you'll find that they will be speaking to you on Monday morning." I had always said that if I was found out I would either kill myself or go AWOL. I was devastated and left the bar to drive away and crash the car. He came out after me saying that he had only told the police the ship and not named the individual. He had also done this with a false name – he had pretended to be a civilian policeman doing them a favour. I had to go back with him again – we had to stay together because I couldn't risk getting him angry – he said he'd call the SIB again.

'I found out that he'd been down to Portsmouth and met with a regulating petty officer [RPO] – and he said he'd been doing it to help me! I just kept trying to appease him.

'The SIB wrote a letter to the captain, which as his secretary I opened and read. They said the allegations about someone on the ship had been made, but that there was not enough evidence to do anything.

'I was effectively a prisoner for the rest of my naval career. He went through my address book and rang up people to ask about me, including former lovers to find out what I had done with them in bed. I made one very big mistake with him, and that was to tell him about a sailor on the ship I was attracted to. I knew that the man was straight, married and had children, and that nothing would ever happen. I never mentioned the fact that I found him attractive to him, and had no intention of doing so. It was no different to male colleagues fancying a woman colleague – but stupidly I told David about him.'

David Varney wrote three anonymous postcards to this man, a petty officer (PO) in June 1993 saying how much the writer was in love with him.

'They were very childish. "I love you" type letters, and as we had Wrens on board I initially thought that he would think they were from one of them. A week later Varney phoned the SIB again and told them the name of the PO I was attracted to, and that he had received some cards. So the link was made between the cards and the rumour that he had started with the SIB about a gay on board. We were at sea when the SIB came on board by boat transfer to investigate. I was terrified, sweating and unsure what was going to happen. I was one of the flight deck officers directing the helicopters landing on the flight deck that night, and I was doing the job whilst concentrating on something else entirely. I destroyed all the letters and things I had in Varney's handwriting on board because they would have matched the handwriting on the postcards.

'By the end of July 1993 I was in a panic. The PO that I had quite liked was still around of course and I completely ignored him. I was probably quite rude to him, but I made a point of not being interested in him. The really stupid thing that I did was to photocopy his photograph from his personnel file to have something to remember him by.

'I subsequently found out that at the end of September Varney had rung the ship and talked to the PO that I had fancied, and talked to him for an hour and a half saying that he was concerned about someone on the ship who was very in love with him. He told the PO that the individual was so in love that he was suicidal about the situation, and the PO told him that although he wasn't gay he didn't think it was serious enough for someone to kill themselves over. I had been suicidally depressed – but certainly not over the PO. The situation with David had depressed me so much that I had spent hours on the flight deck thinking about jumping off. He tried to pretend to be a policeman when he was talking to the PO and arranged a meeting with him outside the gates of the dockyard. David taped the call and I later got a copy of it from him. Fortunately David was late for the meeting and they never met. But at the time of the call I knew nothing about it, I just saw the PO go into the regulating office and close the door and I knew that something else had happened. I got worried again.'

In the middle of October 1993 Graeme bought a flat in

Guildford, and David managed to ensure that he moved in too. At the end of October Graeme's parents came to see the new flat. They were actually going to stay in a hotel in Guildford, but Graeme told Varney that they were going to stay at the flat so that he could get him out for a while. Varney became upset at being forced out of 'his home' and when he started crying and getting angry again, Graeme felt that he had no choice but to give in and let him stay.

'All the time I had to keep giving in to try and keep him happy and stable.

'On one of the nights while they were there, my parents went back to the hotel early and didn't want to go out for the evening. I told David that I was with my parents and went to London to see some friends. I wasn't normally allowed to see other people at all. At about eleven in the evening I drove off the A3 at Guildford and at the top of the slip road David was waiting in his car. He had phoned my parents' hotel and found that they were in their room and deduced that I had gone to London and driven down to confront me. I stopped in the next lay-by and he came over to the car very angry and took my keys from the ignition, held his phone and said he was going to phone the SIB. I had to beg him not to and say that I was sorry.

'I was having to commute from Portsmouth to Guildford every day that I could, and if I said that I had to be at work he would phone people up and ask. He phoned me on board the ship all the time, when I was sitting in the office with my three staff. He had found out about a friend I had and when he opened a letter from him he phoned me on board to say, "Give me one good reason why I shouldn't trash your flat."

'He found the letter from my friend in the glove compartment of my car, where I had hidden it because I knew I couldn't leave a letter from a friend in my flat because he routinely searched everywhere for evidence that I was being "unfaithful" or dishonest. He waved the piece of paper with the phone number he had managed to find in my face and shouted "Choose him or me." I took the number from him and he went hysterical, screaming at me to give it back and started trying to fight me for it. I refused, but then he picked up the phone and said he was going to call the police. I put it down and he grabbed a carving knife and waved it at me and then pointed it at his chest. I managed to calm everything down by saying that I would write to my friend and tell him that I would never see him again.'

But, as he did with many individuals in Graeme's address book, David Varney did phone Graeme's friend, and when the friend denied knowing him Varney threatened to tell his family and employer that he was gay in order to make the friend talk.

'After the New Year I was travelling up and down to Scotland to see my father, who was in hospital dying – although at that time we thought he was going to recover. While I was in Scotland, David phoned me up and said that he was leaving and going back to his flat in Waterloo – he took most of his things with him, although for the next couple of months he kept bringing them back and removing them again as his moods changed.

'Over the months that I had been based at Portsmouth I had been to the gym and swimming pool at the physical training centre at HMS *Temeraire*. I had seen a guy there, at the end of 1993, who I thought was interested in me. I later found that he was an able seaman from another ship. However, there was absolutely no question that I would have approached him at all, in ordinary circumstances.

'On 2 February 1994 I got a phone call in the middle of the night on board from my mother to tell me that my father had died. Of course, I didn't phone David, but I was extremely depressed and had no one that I could really write or talk to about it. David had ensured that for the last year I had barely kept in contact with any other friends. I was extremely upset and depressed and not thinking straight at all. I had to go up to Edinburgh, but I wrote a letter to the guy from the gym first. It was a very stupid thing to do, but I needed to express myself to someone. This letter prompted an investigation, but I was on my way to Edinburgh. I wrote the anonymous letter that really screwed things up for me on the day that my father died, within hours of getting the news. I was under a lot of pressure.'

Graeme went home to Guildford, took a taxi to the airport and flew to Edinburgh. David Varney phoned the ship and found that he wasn't on board, phoned Guildford, found that he wasn't there, and eventually phoned the local mini-cab firm and spoke to the driver who had taken Graeme to the airport. The driver said that his father had died and that he'd gone to Edinburgh. David phoned him in Scotland and demanded to see him. Graeme said no, but a couple of weeks later when Graeme was *en route* to Guildford, David met him from the underground at Waterloo station.

'I hadn't told him that I was on the train, but when I got to Waterloo and came up the escalator he was there waiting. He started shouting at me across the concourse, "You're dead, Lieutenant Ross, you're dead." He was shouting my name and rank around and he followed me on to the train and got in the compartment with me. He emptied my rucksack on to the train floor and started going through everything shouting, "Where've you been?" He hit me and although I could quite easily have killed him I didn't. I tried to calm him down again, and we got off the train at Woking and went back to London. He calmed down and insisted on driving me down to the ship.'

David's obsessive determination to keep control over Graeme reached an even more bizarre level when Graeme hired a car in Portsmouth to drive straight to Edinburgh and see his mother without going via Guildford. While in Scotland, Graeme drove his mother on a long journey to see some relatives. David was unhappy about this, and after Graeme's return phoned the car-hire company to check the mileage, which was a couple of hundred miles more than he would have expected. David confronted Graeme about where he had been.

Graeme was expecting to move to the Falklands for his next appointment at the end of June 1994, but at the end of the first week in April he was told that he was going to have to go to the South Atlantic as soon as possible, as the officer he was replacing had had an accident. He had to prepare to hand over his position on HMS *Manchester* immediately to a replacement. This process, which would normally take several weeks to prepare for, meant that Graeme had to work over the weekend. David kept phoning him on board and demanded that he go up to see him in Guildford on the Saturday 'or else'.

Graeme drove up to Guildford, as he had to see an estate agent to arrange to let his flat while he was in the Falklands. He used this as an excuse to get his door keys back from David.

'I went back to the ship and he rang me to check that I was there. On Monday 18 April there was a pipe that I had a phone call. It was him and he said that I should call him back immediately. I did, with a fifty-unit phone card, and he said that he had found someone I knew from Newcastle. I thought he was talking about the city of Newcastle, but he was being deliberately cryptic and obtuse. I had met a gay lieutenant-commander from HMS *Newcastle* a year or so earlier on two occasions and had no recollection whatsoever of speaking about him to David. But at the time of the call I didn't make the connection at all, I didn't even think of Duncan on HMS *Newcastle*, and I didn't know what David was talking about.

'We had a long and difficult discussion and I used up the phone card completely. The next day, Tuesday, I was piped to the first lieutenant's office, where the master at arms, and two SIB officers in suits were waiting for me. They said that they wanted to talk to me about my homosexuality. Everything just sort of died then. I said OK and they wanted to go to the SIB office at HMS *Nelson*. I had to go to the ship's office to get my cap, and I was accompanied by them as they didn't trust me on my own.'

Graeme was interviewed and spoke honestly, if somewhat heatedly, about David Varney and the situation he had been in. The SIB responded by taking him back to the ship to search his cabin. They took a lot of items which, by October 1994, six months later, had not been returned. The items taken were not listed, but included a copy of *Gay Times*, the cassette tape of Varney's phone call with the petty officer which was in Graeme's briefcase, and a condolences card signed by all the seamen in his department on the loss of his father, which was viewed as suspicious because all the names were men. Anything with a phone number was taken, as was the photocopied photograph of the petty officer.

'It all made everything seem so sordid. When I came back to the ship I saw my Head of Department and the first lieutenant and they tried to be helpful, but I was close to tears and nearly broke down. The captain said he was still my divisional officer and to let him know if I needed any help. In fact I spent that first night with him and his wife in Petersfield. It was very good of them, but next morning I arrived back on board at one minute to Colours walking behind the captain, with two watches standing on the flight deck watching. My job included responsibility for all the money that is held on board, about thirty-thousand pounds, and I had to hand the money and the confidential documents over to my relief. I went to bed at about eight o'clock feeling awful, my throat was closing and I could hardly breathe, so I was taken to the sickbay at Haslar [the Royal Navy's hospital in Portsmouth], and stayed there.'

Meanwhile the story of the second career that David Varney was to destroy was reaching its climax. Somehow he had found out that the head of the supply department on HMS *Newcastle*, Lieutenant-Commander Duncan Lustig-Prean was also gay. He cannot have possibly known more than Duncan's Christian name and unit from Graeme, although Graeme has no recollection of ever talking about him at all.

Sometime in December 1993 David Varney had written an anonymous letter to Duncan's captain telling him that Duncan was gay, and was giving other officers AIDS. Duncan's captain did not act on this letter at the time, saying later that he had no intention of acting on malicious anonymous letters about officers on board his ship.

On 9 June 1994 Duncan received a call from his mother saying that someone called 'David' had called three times telling him to call about something very urgent, but not to call from the ship. Although Duncan had never heard of David, he had an awful premonition about what it was all about. After all, Duncan lives with Martin, who has been his partner for three years.

'I called him on his mobile number from a phone away from the ship and I was very cagey and circumspect. He said we should get together in London, and that it was about an SIB investigation. I was very worried about being set up, but agreed to meet him at midnight at Waterloo station. I cleared everything from my cabin that could be considered incriminating and went to meet him.

'I wandered around and "cased the joint" at the station, and this big bloke came towards me with a phone/radio in his back pocket and I thought I'd been caught by navy policemen. But he said he was a friend of Graeme's, and knew details about him. He knew that we served in the same destroyer squadron, and other details, so I listened to him. But his story did not ring true. He said that the SIB had my name but no evidence, and that he was warning me off so that I could take steps to hide the fact that I was gay. He talked to me for about two hours, walking on the Embankment. He talked about Graeme as though they had been great lovers, but the way he was describing him as violent and difficult was clearly not true. I did not trust him at all. When I left I still had incriminating evidence on me like photographs of my boyfriend. I buried them on the way back to Portsmouth and went back on board and worried – and then drove home. I was aware of surveillance techniques and took account of them. I had to decide whether this was the right time to come out, or to bluff it out. I didn't think that my life would stand up to a really close investigation, and had been worried about security vetting for a possible job with the Prime Minister's office anyway. By Friday evening I had decided to face it.

'Over the weekend we went and saw my boyfriend's gay cousin and talked it over with him. We spoke to gay groups like Stonewall and Rank Outsiders and I decided to come out. I had always said that when the time came I would be open and say yes I'm gay, look at my record. I had never really covered up, and the veneer was very thin.'

Duncan was sure that if he didn't come out he would open himself up to blackmail from David Varney.

'I have no doubt whatsoever that if I hadn't come out I would be paying him money now.'

On Monday Duncan went back to his ship and phoned the head of SIB at HMS *Nelson* and arranged to see him 'on a matter of some importance'. He then spoke to his captain who was surprised but not shocked. When Duncan explained the circumstances his captain said, 'You don't have to do this.' Duncan believes that his captain did not want him to throw away his very successful career.

'I went to the SIB and saw Lieutenant-Commander Slade. As soon as I said the word gay he stopped me and cautioned me. He was very polite and said that he would have to conduct the interview properly. It lasted about twenty minutes. They asked me about other servicemen, and I told them nothing. They asked me if I liked anal intercourse, and so I asked them about what they liked to do in bed and gave them a lecture on AIDS and the reality that homosexuality does not automatically mean buggery. They asked if I minded them searching my cabin. I said that I did because I was not going to let them undermine all the work I had put into rebuilding my department by them walking in like that and going through everything. It would destroy confidence in my department. I also told them that since my admission was voluntary they must be mad if they thought that I would have left anything incriminating in my cabin. They phoned my captain and he was fully supportive – he did not want the ship to become aware of the reason. I spent two more days on board finishing up – but as soon as I got back the public money was taken off me.'

Duncan went on 'compassionate leave while awaiting re-appointment' and was told that everything should take six to eight weeks. Soon afterwards he received a phone call from his appointer asking him to go and take up a post as assistant chief of staff (Policy and Planning) at Fleet Headquarters in Northwood. Duncan questioned how he could be employed when he was being sacked for being unemployable, and was told that the Commander-in-Chief Fleet and the Royal Navy's chief judge advocate saw no reason why, as a homosexual, he shouldn't be employed at a shore establishment.

'I wanted to spend the time trying to find a new job and contacted my captain. He went up to see the people at the Ministry of Defence and lobbied for me, also saying that he thought my discharge was unjustified and unfair. I told my appointer that I would do the job if ordered to, but would make a formal complaint about it. I wanted to leave the navy with my reputation intact, not as a broken reed waiting to be thrown out, in a shore job.'

Duncan went on leave and received no letter, phone call or visit from the Royal Navy for 135 days. In fact, he only heard from the navy when he contacted them to ask advice about talking to the press.

He has received letters from the ship from all ranks and rates, which were wholly supportive. One, from a previously homophobic able seaman aged seventeen, said that he wanted Duncan back as his boss. He also got a phone call from the Mess secretary asking where to send his leaving tankard. Before Duncan left the ship he had decided to tell his senior NCOs what had happened.

'I have never seen six grown men, aged thirty-five to forty-five cry before. One chief looked at my photo of me with the Queen on the bulkhead and said he had always known there was more than one queen in it. They said they had guessed years ago and it didn't matter.'

Meanwhile Graeme's problems with David Varney were still continuing. At the beginning of 1994 Varney had joined the Royal Naval Reserve, as an ordinary seaman, aged thirty-three, in order to get closer access to individuals and information through possessing an identity card. He succeeded. While Graeme was in the Royal Navy hospital at Haslar, he tried to track him down. He finally managed to by getting his secretary to impersonate a woman police officer and telephone Graeme's sister. The secretary said that she had information about a broken window on Graeme's car from several months earlier and needed to contact Graeme. It worked.

Graeme's sister told him that he was in the hospital at Haslar, and so, using his new identity card, David went to visit.

'I couldn't believe he was there. I managed to get my back door key off him and some photos, but he still has lots of my personal possessions. He told me that he had nothing to do with me being caught! I have seen his original statement to SIB and it is three-quarters demonstrably untrue. He says that I was taking drugs and violent towards him. The SIB kept calling him an ordinary seaman in their reports, which makes it look as though I was taking advantage of him, despite the fact that he was thirty-three, had been in the RNR a matter of a couple of months, and had joined with the express purpose of increasing his ability to get information about me and other people in the service.

'During the summer he came down to my flat and started trying to break in. I called the police and then went out to talk to him. He did eight hundred pounds' worth of damage to my car and was arrested. I started receiving nuisance calls and had BT arrange for a tracing facility. The calls were traced to a Mercury mobile phone owned by his company. When the police interviewed him he said that someone else in the office must have had the number, but after that the phone calls stopped. He has repeatedly threatened to go to the press and make up stories about me taking secret documents and abusing sailors and anything he thinks of at the time.'

The most alarming aspect of the situation is the fact that through his connections David Varney must have uncovered information about other lesbian and gay servicemen. What is he doing to them now? In his letter to Duncan's commanding officer David mentions another serviceman by his Christian name – neither Duncan nor Graeme has any idea who he is, but clearly David Varney does.

If there were no ban on lesbians and gay men serving in the British armed forces then Graeme would simply have told David Varney to get lost. Duncan would have refused to meet him and would be continuing his career in one of the three top jobs for someone of his rank and branch. Graeme's record was also very good, and he had thought about applying to transfer to the Royal Marines. The ban is itself the grounds for the blackmail. As it is, Duncan is to be sacked as a homosexual, and Graeme for misconduct – for writing the letter on the day his father died to a junior seaman. No account seems to have been taken in examining these cases of the role played by David Varney.

In fact, an unhealthy relationship seems to have been built up between an unstable emotional blackmailer and the SIB. It appears that David Varney has been courted by them over a period of time in order to help them uncover details of serving homosexuals.

When I spoke to the Ministry of Defence I asked them about the techniques used by the service police to investigate homosexuality. Their spokesman said policemen were notoriously difficult to control and that they set their own agenda. Unfortunately, at the moment, it is this police agenda that is causing the security problems.

7

STAYING IN THE CLOSET

THE LAST FEW years have seen lesbian and gay issues
thrown into the mainstream media spotlight – the age of consent debate, in particular, received a huge amount of media
coverage. Prominent features and editorials in the press
argued the pros and cons of the case, and it would have been
difficult to have arranged for more representatives of the
lobbying group Stonewall and other lesbian and gay figures to
appear on daytime television 'people' shows, and radio talk-
ins. Straight or gay, interested or not, the whole of Britain has
been reading about lesbian and gay rights increasingly often.
Those opposed to change have spoken of the 'gay political
mafia', and of 'homosexual propogandists' forcing their
agendas on to the media – and it's certainly true that in the
last few years lesbians and gay groups have become more successful and organised in their approach to the media and
politicians. As a result, lesbian and gay issues have become a
greater part of the mainstream political agenda.

Two major surveys into sexual behaviour in Britain, by
Sigma and the Wellcome Foundation, reported in 1994, and
although they differed in some of their findings, they both
demonstrated clearly that there is a large active gay and lesbian community in Britain. It is probably true that it has
never been easier for ordinary men or women to describe
themselves openly as lesbian or gay. In cosmopolitan, middle-
class Britain, homosexuality is no longer seen as the disease or
psychiatric problem that it once was – and many 'out' lesbians and gays 'wear' their sexuality with pride. The World

Health Organisation removed homosexuality from its list of psychiatric diseases in 1989 and no major Western Government health department views homosexuality as either an 'illness' or 'curable' any more.

London's annual Gay Pride march, one of a number now held in Britain, is staged close to the anniversary of the Stonewall riots in New York on 26 June 1969, and attracts upwards of 100,000 men and women – many of them bringing heterosexual friends, families and children with them. It is the largest march through the streets of London every year, except perhaps for the Lord Mayor's Show, and culminates in an enormous outdoor 'event' in a London park with a funfair, outdoor concert and firework display. We are living in a society where it is increasingly possible to be completely open about one's homosexuality, where individuals like Sir Ian McKellen, Michael Cashman, and MPs Chris Smith and Michael Brown, Congressman Gerry Studds, actress Pam St Clements and tennis star Martina Navratilova appear in newspapers and television interviews as openly lesbian and gay.

For lesbians and gays in the armed forces, watching this revolution, watching the increasingly open nature of civilian lesbian and gay lifestyles, the frustrations of having to remain in the closet are enormous.

Of course, many can't do it – Royal Navy radio operator Robbie MacGillivray came out because he was filled with indignation at being unable to be open about his sexuality. Any serviceman or woman who is fully conscious of, and happy with, his or her homosexuality must find it difficult to cope with remaining in the closet solely for the sake of their job in a society that talks more and more openly about homosexuality. But many men and women continue to lead double lives, and serve in all the armed forces, knowing they are gay.

Jason is an NCO in an intelligence branch of one of the armed forces. He has been serving for nearly ten years.

'I joined the army almost straight from school, although I worked in a supermarket for a while before I was accepted. I had a girlfriend while I was at school, and I had been sleeping with her since I was fourteen – but we finished while I was working at the supermarket. I started seeing another girl who worked in the shop, but although everyone thought we were sleeping together, we never really had sex – I couldn't do it.

'After my basic training, which was alongside all the other recruits and not just those going into intelligence, I started feeling uncomfortable about not having a proper girlfriend. When we started our specialist training almost half the guys were married, and everyone seemed to be engaged to a girl. I know now why I found the situation really uncomfortable, but if someone had called me gay then I would have hit them.

'I went back home on leave and proposed to the girl I had been seeing when I was at school. She took me back and so we were engaged – it was an exciting step for her, and I went back to the unit feeling like one of the lads. We went out and celebrated my engagement. Any worries I had about being gay were pushed right to the back of my mind. We got married six months later – and it was great. You are not really treated as a man by the army until you get married, it's like the transition between being a boy and a man, part of growing up.

'I'm still married, and I guess it's quite a happy marriage, although I think my wife suspects I'm gay – but she'd never say anything. I have to be really careful about meeting blokes – I have been taught about surveillance, and I always treat going cruising or to a pub on the odd occasion as though I'm on the ground, as though I'm being watched.'

Jason has thought long and hard about the risks his double life pose for him and says he has decided that if he is ever properly investigated, or if someone tries to blackmail him, he will admit that he is gay immediately. One can only hope that he would. If the situation were to arise he would be forced to risk his career and family, rather than pay a blackmailer in cash, favours or worse – like Royal Navy Lieutenant Graeme Ross.

Jason has tried very hard to keep his sexuality a complete secret, from his family as well as his colleagues. He doesn't really have any gay friends, although he keeps in casual touch with two or three gay men he has met over the years. Other gay servicemen take a different approach to their sexuality. Chris, a serving sergeant in the RAF, 'came out' in 1993 and has decided to live a 'normal', open gay life in his private time. He has developed an almost 'devil-may-care' attitude to the possibility of discovery.

'If I get caught, then I get caught. I'm not going to live my life missing out and then spend the rest of my life regretting what I missed out on. I'm going to go to bars and clubs and meet guys and have relationships and see what happens.'

Chris has not been caught, and to the best of his knowledge has never been investigated for homosexuality. After about six years of service he has created a lifestyle that allows him to continue to work while living a privately gay life.

For the lesbian or gay man who is serving in Britain's armed forces, there are now more social venues which are easily accessible. Even the most far-flung of our army camps and naval and air bases are within reach of a gay or 'mixed' pub or night club. Plymouth has pubs and clubs; Portsmouth has Drummonds and a couple of night clubs; Aberdeen has several gay pubs and a telephone helpline; Beddgelert in North Wales has the Saracen's Head Hotel (on a Tuesday); Penzance has The Studio. The SAS are catered for by a hotel in Worcester, and the SBS have a wide range of gay clubs, pubs and saunas available to them in Bournemouth, should they desire them.

With such a range of available social life, many lesbians and gay men in the armed forces, like Chris, have found themselves living a strangely divided life: 'out' in private to families and friends, with an active gay social life, and completely closeted at work.

Chris started his military career while he was still 'in the closet' to himself, and he talks fluently and openly about this 'coming out' and how he came to be in his current position.

'When I was younger I had quite a lot of sex with guys in school and around at home – but it wasn't serious really, just playing around. I had quite a lot of girlfriends too. But I think that I joined the RAF to get away from dealing with gay feelings I was having at home. I'd always wanted to fly, so the

RAF was a sensible place to go. I'd never been to bed properly with a man – but I knew I was gay. I'd bought a copy of *Euroboy*, a gay magazine, and hidden it under my bed at home. I finally gave it away to a friend I knew was gay. Everyone knew he was gay, and I just went to him and said, "I know what people say about you" and gave him the magazine. We played around sexually a bit – but I really got away from all that by joining the RAF.'

Some men and women join the armed forces in an attempt to 'straighten up': they believe that they will grow up and out of a homosexual phase once they are part of the competitive heterosexual environment of the army, navy or air force. There must be many who have experienced some homosexual feelings during their adolescence and for whom the military environment provides the 'straight' role model they seek, but for many others the heterosexual emphasis only confirms for them that they are different. Although they can point to events or feelings during their schooldays that should have given them clues, the commonest experience amongst the men and women I spoke to seems to be a self-discovery which took place some time after joining up. Chris is an example.

'I did not think I was gay, not for a couple of years after I joined. One evening I was having a shave when a really nice guy walked into the bathroom completely naked. I found him incredibly sexy, and despite all the denying I knew then that I was still gay and that it wasn't going to go away. I still work with him and he is a really good friend. He's married now and doesn't know that I'm gay – he thinks I'm a womaniser. Nothing has ever happened between us, and nothing ever would – but thinking the way I did confirmed for me that I was gay.

'But I carried on trying to put thoughts of being gay to the back of my mind and started sleeping with girls again. I used to invite them back and then pretend to be too pissed to do anything. Sometimes I'd get off with them and have sex, but it was mostly flirting, a hands-off approach. I'm still like that, lots of flirting and kissing, although I haven't taken it further than that for at least eighteen months now.'

But Chris ultimately found the urge to 'come out' too strong to resist. As others have experienced in the 1990s, there is just too much pressure from a publicly gay community in Britain – and Australia and the United States. Chris found himself confronting the issue more often.

'On leave, a friend from London came down sometimes when my parents were away, and we played around a bit, but it still wasn't serious. Then two friends I knew were gay invited me round when they had some friends staying. I was really nervous, particularly because one of them kept looking at me and I knew what was going on. I said that I had to go home, and he came with me. It happened naturally, but I was really nervous, all my feelings were released at once and I was able to do what I had wanted to do and fantasised about. We got up in the morning and I dropped him off before going flying.

'I was on a high, not in a panic at all, and the guys said I looked as though I'd been shagging. I went to Leeds to see the guy again and it started to be a relationship, although it turned quite quickly into a friendship. Whenever I go to see him now I stay in the spare room and we go out to check out the talent together. Last time I was there he gave me my own key the night before in case I didn't make it home!'

At the moment Chris seems to have found a way of living his life that allows him the best of both worlds. One of his non-service gay friends now believes that Chris's time in the RAF is limited. He says it must be becoming more and more obvious that Chris is gay to his colleagues, and that as he becomes part of a lesbian and gay community outside the armed forces he will inevitably become more political and want to stand up for his rights. This certainly happens to some individuals – RAF Corporal Ian Waterhouse, was discharged in 1994 after being spotted at the 1993 Gay Pride March in London. But Chris thinks he can make it work, for the time being.

'None of the guys at work know that I'm gay – I've still got a womanising reputation. One of the girls called me a tart and it's stuck. I travel a long way to go out for weekends and I

117

stay with gay friends. When I meet someone in a bar I lie about what I do. I've been a bricklayer and a vet – I try to work out how intelligent they are before I say what I do – I always ask them first.

'It gets difficult, but if I see them again then I tell them what I do. They ask where you are from and I pick somewhere a long way away. I can't have a relationship; the closest I get is on the phone or by post. I tend to have just one- or two-night stands. There is one guy who writes and I see him when I'm on leave.

'I'd like to have a relationship with some of the guys I've met, but I need to keep them away – some offer to come down here to see me and I have to put them off. My job is too important to me to risk losing it so easily. The job is exciting, I get to visit lots of places and I get a good wage. I love my job. I signed up for twelve years, which is the minimum required for aircrew. I can get out after eight years and I probably will – I can prepare for that. If I wasn't gay then I would definitely stay on – and if they change the rules then that would persuade me to stay too. Even "Don't ask – Don't tell" would be better than the situation at the moment.

'I don't know how my colleagues would react if they knew that I was gay, shock I suppose, although I guess some wouldn't be that surprised. Things might fall into place for them – I spend a lot of time in the bathroom and get called vain, for example, before we go out to a nightclub.

'Obviously when someone does get thrown out, and a few have recently, the guys talk about it quite a lot. Much of the comments are along the lines of, "He was a nice guy, good at his job." I'm quite popular and I suppose that the same would be true of me. I'm very patriotic and proud of my roots; I would have no qualms at all about fighting for my country. I would be proud to.'

But, what about the showers? The argument for lifting the ban always comes up against the same obstacle. How would you like to share your showers with a poof? How does Chris manage?

'The stereotypes are so stupid, all the stuff about sharing

showers. I've been in the squadron football team for years and we share showers and changing rooms all the time. They're colleagues and I'm not looking at them to fancy them. Not many of the team are cute anyway, one or two are worth looking at I suppose, but we all bundle into the changing rooms and I can quite happily switch off and go into the showers.

'0898 telephone sex numbers offer the fantasy of sharing a shower with a bunch of fit military men. I know it's a very sexy image, but I do it once a week and I never get a hard on. In the shower I don't look, I just concentrate on washing my hair.'

Chris's experiences of coping as an NCO who has decided to try to live as normal a life as possible show how it can work, at least for a while: it's entirely possible that by the time this book is published Chris will have been found out and dismissed. More senior members of the armed forces find that they have the same dilemmas.

John is a mid-ranking officer in the army who currently holds a desk job at headquarters level. He has spent all of his adult working life as an officer in the army and has commanded large units of soldiers in Britain and abroad. Although he now has a staff job he is intending to apply for early retirement so that he can 'enjoy life outside the rather stilted social environment of the army'.

He has 'come out' relatively recently to his family and to a few close friends, and whilst on holiday in Paris in 1993 visited a gay bar for the first time.

'I joined the army instead of going to university – it was all I had ever wanted to do. I remember at school everyone seemed to change their mind about what they wanted from life every fifteen minutes, but I just wanted to be a soldier. During my basic training I tried very hard to conform to the heterosexual stereotype and basically succeeded. I tried relationships with women, but in the long term they didn't work. I suppose I knew that men were what really attracted me quite early on in my career – but it wasn't until quite recently that I had the nerve to do anything about it. If a relationship with a woman didn't work I blamed it on the fact that I was gay – but I didn't think it was acceptable to be homosexual. I used to drink quite a lot, but that wasn't really that unusual at the time.'

Chris and John both explained that they have slept with women solely to reinforce their reputations as heterosexual men. However, these 'relationships' invariably falter at a very early stage – when I visited Milwaukee as a young naval officer in 1987 I found myself cornered into going to bed with a beautiful young American woman after a cocktail party. She was practically throwing herself at me, and I felt that if I said no everyone would want to know why on earth I had let her go.

The following day, very rudely, I stood her up. Bizarrely, the episode only went to reinforce my reputation as heterosexual – wham, bam, thank you ma'am. I am not alone in having entered sexual relationships, and for some even marriages, for what surely must be the wrong reasons. John's failure to marry strengthened his commitment to work.

'I had a lot of sexual energy and frustration which I didn't know how to direct. I was unfulfilled in my personal life and as a result put a lot of energy into achieving success in my job. I did not think that being gay was acceptable – I still find it a problem to be honest – and I thought that the tougher I became as a soldier the less gay I would be. It didn't work for my sex life, but it made me a success in the job.

'All sorts of defence mechanisms started to set themselves up in my life, and I always joined in the homophobic conversations that happened from time to time. I was quite a tough officer, and was told on more than one occasion that I was too hard on my men. I think they respected me, but I always felt that I had something to prove.

'It really wasn't until I sorted out my sexual feelings a bit more – on a holiday with army friends who thought I was seeing a local girl – that I began to relax a bit as an officer.'

Although John has carried on with his career, he has begun to make contact with the fringes of cosmopolitan gay society. He meets people for dinners and drinks, but is always secretive about himself. It is a compromise that allows him a degree of sexual satisfaction, but no real opportunity for a relationship.

Many others, like John, take the option of retiring rather than face the unpleasant possibility of a formal investigation and dismissal. They don't show up in the Ministry of Defence statistics.

Lieutenant-Commander Simon Langley, a Royal Navy officer, took that option. Despite his outstanding record as a Fleet Air Arm pilot and instructor, and his desire to continue his career as a pilot, he had the choice of applying for voluntary redundancy as part of the defence cuts. Rather than wait for what he felt was the inevitable moment when the Royal Navy started investigating him, he applied for retirement, which he was granted.

Simon Langley's was not an atypical childhood for an officer in the armed forces – his father was a serving RAF officer, and sent him to a single-sex boarding school in Bath. By the time he had entered his teenage years he had already reached the conclusion that he was gay, and by the time he left school had experimented with a number of small-scale relationships. When he left school in 1979 he decided to become a helicopter pilot in the navy.

'At the end of 1979 I attended the Admiralty Interview Board and was selected for officer training. I joined Dartmouth in February 1980. To be honest I have no memory of being asked whether or not I was gay at the interviews (that is not to say it did not happen, it's just that I do not remember it). However, having got to Dartmouth, I was quickly made aware of the confidential guidelines and regulations about homosexuality as part of my training in personnel and discipline. It was therefore clear to me that I was in breach of Queen's Regulations. I simply continued to hide my sexuality from the navy.'

Simon passed out from the Royal Naval College at Dartmouth, and after two years qualified as a helicopter pilot. He served in a variety of units, alternately at sea and at the Royal Naval Air Station at Culdrose in Cornwall. In 1987 Simon was selected to become a helicopter instructor and after qualifying became responsible for training new pilots as well as front-line operational pilots. In 1991 he became the solo display pilot for the Royal Navy's internationally known Sharks display team, representing the navy at displays throughout Britain. It was while flying as the navy's number one display pilot that he qualified as an A2 helicopter instructor, the second highest grade possible.

While clearly excelling at his job, Simon Langley had also continued in secret to live his life as a gay man.

'I continued to be active on the gay scene, mainly in London, but the strain was beginning to tell. I was finding it very difficult to balance my sexuality with my job. Several events occurred which caused me to think again about the risks that I was running, and made me decide to resign my commission. Having been active in London, I started to go out on the scene in Plymouth, despite the obvious risk of being caught. It was on the Plymouth scene that I developed the art of creating a false identity to tell my gay friends so that they would not guess my true profession and I would not run the risk of being blackmailed. I hated lying to people, but it was necessary.

'Then, in 1992, a gay friend of mine introduced me to my current partner, Alistair. Not long after a straight friend confronted me with the dreaded question: "Are you gay?" I decided to tell him the truth. It didn't faze him at all, and he remains one of my closest friends. However the fact that he had asked set me thinking – if he could see it, why couldn't the navy? The evidence was fairly damning. In all my thirteen years' career I had never taken a woman to a social function – I either avoided them or attended on my own. I had never had, or talked about, a girlfriend. I avoided homophobic banter. I can only think that my peers were either incredibly stupid or were only concerned that I did my job well – I tend to believe the latter. I therefore decided that, should the question ever arise from someone within the forces, I would no longer lie but would admit my sexuality and show no shame, however naïve that may sound.'

In the end Simon was not caught and left the navy with an unblemished record. However, the fact that he is no longer serving is as directly attributable to the ban as it is to those who are dismissed and do show up in the statistics.

There are gay helicopter pilots like Simon Langley flying in the Royal Navy still, and I have met other serving officers like John whilst researching this book. It is apparent to anyone who lives in Portsmouth, Aldershot, Aberdeen, Worcester or Bournemouth, or any of the other towns and cities with lesbian and gay businesses throughout Britain, that the 260 personnel dismissed for homosexuality between 1990 and 1994 represent only a small proportion of the lesbians and gays still serving amongst the 300,000 members of the British armed forces. It was while visiting a gay bar in one of the eastern counties of England that I met Yvonne, a captain in a technical regiment of the army. She was out for the evening with her girlfriend and was happy to talk to me over the telephone the following day, but she did not want to meet again.

'There is always a risk that I'm going to get caught. I think that most of my women colleagues know I'm gay, and there's not much I can do about that. Many of them are gay themselves, and those that aren't don't make an issue about it. Some other women officers do not like the fact that there are lesbians around, but they tolerate us – I don't think any of them would deliberately report you. We all try to respect each other's differences.

'I think that maybe it's easier to be a gay woman in the forces than to be a gay man – there are a lot of us, and between the women it can be quite obvious who is gay. Maybe that's the same with the men, but I think they feel the need to hide it more. But that ignores the difficulty women have being in the army in the first place.

'I know it's a cliché to say that it is a male environment, but it is true – this is not the place for traditional women's skills. I know that we have a lot to offer the army, but management is only just beginning to realise that. We have still got a long way to go to prove ourselves in the eyes of the men.

'Did I know I was gay when I joined? No, not really. I knew that my relationships with men were never very comfortable. I had a series of relationships with men while I was at university, but they were never really successful. They were all sexual relationships – I think I kept trying to find a man who really made me feel comfortable in bed. Whenever we were having sex I kind of switched off. My mind was one step removed from what was going on and I felt like I was watching myself, waiting to let go and really relax.'

Like many men and women in the armed forces, Yvonne was introduced to the truth about her sexuality whilst serving.

'I sometimes wonder if I would ever have come to terms with being gay if I hadn't been in the army. Once you realise what is going on there are so many good role models for gay women in the armed forces. There are women that you know, or find out, are lesbians, and some of them are very high up and obviously very good at their jobs. In my first Mess there was one very attractive woman who made it clear that she wasn't interested in men, and several of my colleagues said that she was a lesbian. I found the idea fascinating – I'd never really thought that I might be the same before then.

'I kept watching her and finally spoke to her, and said that I thought I might be gay too. She took me out and we talked about how I was feeling, and I slept at her house. We shared a bed and talked, but nothing sexual happened, although the atmosphere was very sexual. I don't think she fancied me, but I woke up in the morning thinking how great it was, and how I wanted to have a woman to wake up next to all the time.

'She took me to my first gay bar, and I was really surprised when she told other people in the Mess where we were going. But because the bar is known for gays people didn't think about lesbians going there. She told people that she liked the atmosphere and wanted to know that she wasn't going to be hassled by male officers or soldiers by going to the normal clubs. People accepted that!

'I felt terrified going into the bar, which is more of a night club really, but once you're in there you sort of melt into the feeling of the place. There were not many women there – but they seemed to stare at me all the time. I think it's quite a small community and they notice outsiders. One or two of them knew my friend, and we started talking. When I found that one of them was in the army as well I got very nervous. But by the end of the evening I had had so much fun – I knew that this was what I wanted to be. I liked the fact that the men just kind of disappeared into the background, it's like they're not there – totally different from a straight club where they're in your face the whole time.

'When we left and drove back my friend seemed really pleased that I was so happy, and she told me that one of the women had fancied me – and made me try to guess which one. It was one that I hadn't really paid a lot of attention to. But I felt excited that someone, a woman, had said that she found me sexually attractive. I found that very exciting.'

When Yvonne moved to a different base, her friend, who was more senior, told her the names of two lesbian women in her new Mess. Yvonne introduced herself as a friend of so-and-so, and was immediately introduced to other gay women at the base.

'I had still not actually been to bed with another woman although I knew that I was a lesbian. If a witch-hunt had happened then, I would have lost my job despite the fact that I had done nothing at all – but I would have been in people's diaries and letters as gay. My new colleagues took me to the only bar that was within realistic travelling distance and I met a group of local women, many of whom worked as civilians on the bases. One night when we were out I met a friend of one of them who was visiting from London, and we just started talking and talking and looking at each other. I'm from London too, and we had a lot in common. She's a civil servant. At the end of the evening we exchanged numbers and kissed. I phoned her the next day, and went to stay with her the next weekend in London. That was nearly two years ago and we are still together.'

I asked Yvonne if she felt that the pressure of leading a double life, rushing off to London at every opportunity, affected her ability to do her job effectively and well.

'I think the army has always believed that an officer or soldier with a stable relationship will be more secure in themselves and able to concentrate on their work. The system itself encourages marriage, which I think is right – fast living, hard drinking soldiers with unstable relationships are no use to anyone. Of course many army marriages fail, but the army does try to support the wives, and to some degree the husbands. Marriage is an old-fashioned institution, but then so is the army, and the two are compatible. What I would like to see is the same respect given to my partner. She provides for me the same stability and happiness and understanding of myself that a husband would if I was straight. She contributes to my ability to serve as a good officer – and she should have that recognition. I'm not ashamed of her – and I wish that I could bring her to more army functions. She has come to some things as a "friend", but I actually find that very difficult because I start getting annoyed that I can't introduce her properly, and she gets angry because I'm not being open about us. We've always ended up having an argument afterwards.'

At every stage of their career, Yvonne, Chris, John and Jason risk it all coming to an abrupt end. Sometime in the future they will probably weigh it all up and decide to leave while they still can.

In preparing this book I spoke to one very senior officer who is married and, very hesitantly, agreed to make some comments about his own homosexuality.

'I followed the proper pattern in the 1950s and got married. There was no question whatsoever of announcing your homosexuality – in fact it was not until many years later that I would have listened to that label without hating it. The fact that I was close to a number of men had nothing to do with homosexuality in my mind then.

'Even now my wife is the most important thing in my life, and my children. But I suppose I wish that I could have done things differently. I have, when abroad, on occasion visited "gay" bars and met friends. But now when I walk into one of those bars the young men look at me and see what I am – an old man. I cannot tell you how much I regret that I was not able to meet people when I was a young man. I was a very attractive young officer, but I have missed out completely on that part of my life. I will continue to serve until they tell me to retire, and I don't imagine that anyone will ever really know what I missed out on – except me.

'I wish you the best of luck with the book. You can tell people that homosexuals can serve, often better, than heterosexuals, but I often wish I had left before now. Until the rules change, and I'm afraid that may be some time away, I would not recommend people to follow in my footsteps without really thinking about what they are giving up. Unless a senior management career is what you really want, be honest to yourself and leave. I will always regret the fun and relationships I never had, despite my success.'

8

WITH ROSE-TINTED
SPECTACLES?

A NUMBER OF ancient Greek historians wrote about the
Sacred Band of Thebes – an all-gay army of lovers – which
was the ancient Greek equivalent of NATO's élite rapid response units. The Sacred Band was made up of 300 full-time
soldiers who were driven on by a determination never to
appear cowardly in the presence of their lovers. Critics of the
policy at the time suggested that units would be better organised along tribal lines – but General Pammenes, one-time
leader of the Sacred Band, defended the policy of recruiting
lovers:

> For tribesmen and clansmen make little account of fellow
> tribesmen and clansmen in times of danger; whereas, a band
> that is held together by the friendship between lovers is indis-
> soluble and not to be broken, since the lovers are ashamed to
> play the coward before their beloved, and the beloved before
> their lovers, and both stand firm.

The Sacred Band died fighting in 338 BC at Chaeronea,
defending Greece from the invading armies of Philip of Mace-
don. Philip himself had spent three years with the Band as a
fifteen-year-old in 367 BC when he had been held hostage by
the Greeks. After the battle at Chaeronea:

> Philip was surveying the dead, and stopped at the place where
> the 300 were lying, all where they had faced the long spears of
> his phalanx, with their armour, and mingled with one an-
> other. He was amazed, and on learning that this was the band
> of lovers and beloved, burst into tears and said, 'Perish

miserably they who think that these men did or suffered aught disgraceful.'

In the course of preparing this book I spoke to several retired senior officers in the army, navy and RAF who were homosexual and had successful careers. One story stood out. Neil, a retired wing commander who served throughout the Second World War, tells his own story far better than I could hope to.

'I suppose that I had the kind of background you might expect from someone who was going to become a Royal Air Force officer. My Roman Catholic parents sent me to a Roman Catholic school where nearly all the teachers were priests. It was a difficult environment in which to make the discovery that I was attracted to other men, but by the time I was twelve or thirteen I knew that I was homosexual. I had started masturbating and told a priest at confession. He asked if I had masturbated with other boys and I said no – I had made a decision that I was not going to tell the church that I was gay. In fact I found this suggestion that I could do that with other boys quite sexy. The teachers all said that anything sexual with another boy was a mortal sin and I really started to have doubts about the Roman Catholic faith. I knew from reading that there was an alternative point of view and I thought of the religious education as brainwashing. I was a good pupil and won all the academic prizes at the end of terms, but I don't think that the teachers liked me because they knew that I wasn't accepting the faith.

'I suppose that I was a rebel intellectually because I was gay. I knew I was different and this performed an important function as I learnt to question things and lead a secret and resourceful life. Being gay as a young Roman Catholic in the 1930s was not easy – it was a mortal sin. Medically homosexuality was still viewed as a disease, although it was not thought curable then, this was before so-called aversion therapy. So being gay was still a criminal offence, you could be arrested, tried, and sent to prison. It was a sin, a disease and a crime.

'Of course being gay was also grounds for ridicule and

there was a common vein of humour that focused on queers and nancy boys. Being secretive about being gay in the armed forces was not paranoia then, because there really was a group that was out to get you – it was society as a whole. The whole of established society was against you. Take whatever feelings of alienation you have today and multiply them several million times – all you could do was live a secret life and hope.

'I was outed by someone that I had had sex with just after I left school, and my parents were very angry and called in the parish priest. They decided to throw me out and I was given two weeks by my father to leave. I left for London in one week and never saw him again. I saw my mother a couple of times, but a year later they were both killed in a car crash. They had wanted a good little Roman Catholic boy, and I wasn't it – there had never been any affection between us at all.

'In London I shared a flat with a South African flyer and he was much more experienced than me sexually and taught me a lot about sexual technique – I was very naïve then.

' I began to realise that being gay had a lot of advantages – I was an outsider and had never learned to accept second-hand thinking. I wasn't really influenced by my parents, teachers or friends – I thought things through for myself and had an independent mind.

'When I joined the RAF my capacity for independent thought was very useful.

'I applied for a short service commission in the RAF in March 1939 – warclouds were looming – but I would have joined even if there hadn't been a war. I had a sense of adventure and wanted to lead a man's life. I suppose I thought that the RAF would be more modern than the army or navy – maybe less regimented. I was nineteen and I knew that I was one hundred per cent homosexual and that it was forbidden. I went in with my eyes open: I was going to lead a double life.

'I assumed that I would have an active sex life in and out of the RAF. The RAF were slow to call me up and I finally started on 6 September 1939, three days after the outbreak of war. I had a four-year commission initially, but after the war it was made permanent.

'The call-up was very clumsy and there was a mixture of people like myself who had applied before the war and also the reserves who were being called up too. In my Mess there were about sixty of us and we all had experience of working in the outside world, and a lot of the reserves had more worldly experience than the permanent officers who were training us.

'Our commanding officer heard me talking in a debate during the training and asked me to come back as an instructor after my first job.

'So I spent the beginning of the war as part of the training staff for the called-up young officers. A number of them were gay and I could usually tell – I always got it right. I would come out to them and they did to me, and I tried to advise them on how to live a double life. I had become a bit of a role model myself for the young gay officers. I was able to give them warnings about what to avoid – and I had sex with some of them. I didn't think that was unprofessional as these men were generally more experienced and older than me.

'Of course it was a difficult subject to broach with someone – we might go for a country walk and start asking if the other had wives or girlfriends. I remember one in particular: we used to go to concerts in London together and became life-long friends. It would have been total disaster to talk about it openly. All the machinery for the destruction of gay men was there – if you went too close to the edge then you would fall over. Nobody would have dared to say publicly that they were gay – it was supposed to be complete conscription and I am not aware of anyone who said they were gay to get out of it.

'On one occasion while I was stationed in Buckinghamshire I had to go on a long car journey up north and became ill on the way. The driver took me to an RAF station in Lincolnshire to see the medical officer. The MO started to examine me and I noticed that he was absolutely gorgeous. For once I lost control and while I was stripped I got a hard-on.

I said how embarrassed I was and he said not to worry and our eyes met. We had sex on many occasions and he died a few years ago.

'After a couple of years in training I moved into jobs at the Air Ministry in equipment, administration and intelligence. In 1942 and 1943 I was living in London sharing a flat with another gay officer. I was working in a small department under a wing commander, and another flight lieutenant who was also gay. But he was careless and I didn't really trust him. The wing commander found some gay pornography in his desk and denounced him. He had been having sex with NCOs and lower ranks. In my twenty-two years I never had sex with an NCO or other rank. It would have been too dangerous. An NCO might brag, and whereas if I was investigated I would not have been intimidated into naming names an NCO would have been easier to put under pressure to talk.

'But my colleague was careless and it was his downfall. Being gay was something like being a member of the Resistance – a secret, hidden life of continuous danger with your alarm system always primed. On one occasion I was interrogated while they were investigating someone else and they had found my name in his address book. I got a completely clean bill of health, but there were no computers then and if your name came up in more than one investigation it was unlikely to be cross-referenced. They asked me if I thought I was homosexual and I said no.

'In any Officer's Mess on dining-in nights everyone became very drunk and heterosexual and aggressive, asserting their masculinity. The authorities knew that in this state the men would seduce or even rape any woman in the vicinity – there were no real limits on straight male moral conduct – no control on straight sexual conduct at all – and the men would boast of their sexual conquests, and some of them would have constituted rape these days. It was such a double standard because any gay consenting sexual acts were clamped down on.

'The straight problems were covered up too – the officers would be posted away if there were allegations of rape. Meanwhile the parks and streets were humming with all kinds of sex.

'I had to have a strategy of disguise – you had to have camouflage. Many got married, but during basic training I decided on my cover. I had left the Roman Catholic Church and joined the Church of England which I attended regularly. I was, and still am, quite religious. One evening in the Mess we were all quite drunk and someone asked why I never talked about women. I said that I had strong religious beliefs that it was wrong to have sex before marriage, and I was waiting for the right girl to come along. I said that I didn't judge others' conduct, but that I wanted to meet the right girl and still be a virgin (I'm still waiting). My answer caused great mirth, but as they knew I went to church they accepted it.

'During the Battle of Britain I could see the fires burning in London and I went on numerous evenings to Paternoster Row and streets in the City and watched the bombs falling and saw the damage happen. All the Dunkirk evacuees were everywhere on our bases in the south of England and yet even then we didn't feel as though we were going to lose. Churchill's speeches helped, but even without them we would have wanted to win.

'The South African flyer I had been involved with in London was shot down over occupied Europe – and other young gay officers that I had been close to and had sex with were shot down by the Nazis. But I also felt I was at war with the armed forces – as a gay man trying to prove myself. I've always had a burning sense of justice and injustice – and I know that I am entitled to the same rights as heterosexuals.

'In 1944 I was posted to an assistant air attaché job in an embassy in a sensitive neutral country. I learnt the language and became fluent very quickly. I had a responsibility for intelligence work and it would be true to say that the job was sensitive. At the end of the war the ambassador asked for me to stay, and I then had a diplomatic position. I was delighted to find how many other gays there were at the other embassies, particularly the Americans. I had a number of sexual partners, but soon moved in with one, an American naval attaché.

'It was the happiest period of my life, we shared a house for three years and were in love. We had the same sense of humour and outlook and had a very active social life. It was a great love affair, and as we were both diplomats we had three or four dinner parties a week and maybe six cocktail parties to go to. We were often invited together and we entertained ourselves all the time. I remember we had a fancy dress party where everyone had to come as one of the great sinners. Lucrezia Borgia, Hitler and Mae West were all there. The other gays in the diplomatic community knew that we were a couple.

'At one of our parties the British and American ambassadors both came, and at one point the British ambassador made a speech about how good it was for the 'special relationship' for us to be living together. Our friends who were in the know stared at the floor during this memorable speech. The ambassadors had no idea just how 'special' the relationship was.

'For my job here I had to have very high clearance – I knew about the D-Day landings, although not the date. For "Cosmic" Top-Secret clearance I had to answer questions about my sexuality, as did my referees. They gave answers which worked on two levels. The first was that I was deeply religious and wouldn't have sex before marriage – the second level, which I believe that the security people fell for, was the implication that I was really frightened of sex. It worked.

'I remember shortly after the war I accompanied a mission of high-ranking officers from the country to Britain, who, we hoped, were going to buy a lot of military equipment and arms – aeroplanes in particular. I was their escorting officer and interpreter – at that time Government Hospitality was at its best and when the captain who was accompanying the generals asked if partners could be arranged for the generals I said of course and Government Hospitality arranged high-class call-girls for them. One of the generals said he wanted to have me. I said that unfortunately that was impossible and that a male prostitute would have to be found. We provided the delegation of three generals and a colonel with three high-class call-girls and a chap. I spent the night with the captain.

'It was soon after this that I was posted home. I had spent a long time at the embassy, but within days of my return the air attaché and all his staff were killed in a plane crash, and I was told to go back immediately and take over as the senior air attaché. Two major events were planned for the near future, the first visit to the country of a squadron of our jet aircraft, and a tour of the native air force by the British commander-in-chief. I had to prepare for these events single-handed. Each evening during the visit I had to brief the commander-in-chief on the civilian and military figures he was going to meet and debrief on the day just gone, and then prepare for the next function. I then had to accompany him on all the trips, translate for him, and introduce him to politicians and prominent national figures.

'I went to work for the head of the Allied air forces in Europe, an air chief marshal. I served my full time with him dealing with the world's press and advising him on a range of other issues. I have a superb reference from him which says:

I have known the Wing Commander for a number of years. His work, which was of great importance, brought him in almost daily touch with me and I formed a very high opinion of his capabilities.

He possesses a brilliant and well-balanced mind, which he uses to good effect and in a pleasant and unassuming way. He speaks five languages, has travelled much in Europe and the Middle East, has mixed with many nationalities and understands their characteristics, and his work in the Service has brought him into close touch with diplomatic circles.

He has excellent judgement, is decisive and has a quick and penetrating understanding when it comes to dealing with difficult and intricate problems, particularly in the human field. Above all he possesses great integrity, is a tireless worker and has an understanding heart when dealing with other people.

I consulted him and took his advice on many problems when he was on my staff and I found him to be a great philosopher of life and a true and loyal friend. A man who can honestly be placed in the exceptional class. A real winner.

'I received similar letters of commendation from other senior officers. I could clearly have stayed in the RAF for a long career, but when I got to twenty-two years I had the option of retiring and I took it. I had told two senior RAF officers that I was gay, an air commodore and an air-vice-marshal. The air commodore said, "If you are a typical gay then I wish there were more of you," and the air-vice-marshal signed his letter to me when I retired "with admiration"; he said I had been a credit to the RAF.

'I left because although my career was going well, at any time it could all come crashing down. The higher I got the more nervous and cautious I became – you have so much to lose. I'm certain that I would have made at least group captain, but if just one of my sexual partners had given me away I would have lost everything. It would have meant cashiering and court martial. If my sexual activities had come to light there would have been aggressive and intimidating interrogations, a search of my accommodation, medical and psychiatric examinations (the procedure for physical examination of suspects was specified in regulations), pressure to divulge the names of other homosexuals in the service, and everything else that happened when an individual was caught up in the relentless and powerful military machinery, as many hapless gay men were. It could easily have happened to me. There, but for the grace of God ... If I had been court-martialled, not all the commendations from high-ranking officers would have saved me from a prison sentence with all its humiliation and degradation.

'You may find it difficult to visualise what it was like to live in an era in which imprisonment, accompanied by disgrace, was a possibility which could at any time become a reality. I was regularly committing acts ('abominations against nature' etc.) which were punishable by imprisonment. In the middle of a Christmas party, for example, when everyone was in festive mood, I would feel a sudden cold clutch of fear at the heart at the thought that I might be spending the following Christmas in prison. I know that I would have survived in prison, as I am a survivor, but I would have hated it.

'You asked me why, when I made the deliberate choice to apply for a permanent commission and stay on in the RAF after the war, I didn't adopt a celibate way of life. Well, I had a normal healthy sexual appetite. But it was much more than that. I had a burning sense of indignation against the injustice of it all. If I had been celibate it would have been a capitulation to tyranny.

'But once I had qualified for my pension I left – I had had my share of luck, and used up most of my nine lives. I don't think it would have been possible to reach flag rank without a wife anyway. I loved the Royal Air Force and I was very loyal and very sad to leave. But I was relieved that the danger was not hanging over me any more. If it hadn't been for the taboo I would have stayed and they wouldn't have wasted all the time and money they spent on me. I had learnt Russian and spent six months in Paris with a Russian family to make me fluent – but I never really got to use that skill.

'If I had been heterosexual I would have had a conventional life and would have accepted the opinions and views of my superiors. I had learnt to lead a secret life, and that made me a resourceful and independent character. If I were given the choice to live again as a gay or straight I would choose gay. No doubt about it.'

Neil's career, like those of the many thousands like him who have served this century, is part of what is almost a secret history. The enormous majority of lesbians and gay men who have served this country during periods of both war and peace, have done so in complete secrecy. But the details of their careers, and the devotion that they showed to them, are an important part of the story of homosexuality in the British armed forces. Unlike their predecessors in Thebes they served secretly and have no memorial.

At the site of the battle at Chaeronea a large marble monument was erected shortly afterwards. It is still there. During the nineteenth century the base was broken open, and a number of the shields were found inside – on which are inscribed, still legibly, the names of the lovers who had fought together. More recent archaeological investigation has revealed the remains of more than 250 warriors laid out side-by-side in seven rows.

9

WORLDS APART

IF ROYAL NAVY rating Brett Burnell, or RAF Sergeant Simon Ingram, or Army Lieutenant Elaine Chambers had been serving in the armed forces of at least twelve other European countries their careers would not have come to an end. France, Belgium, Austria, Holland, Germany, Finland, Denmark, Ireland, Norway, Sweden, Switzerland and Spain all allow homosexuals to serve openly in their ranks.

The British Ministry of Defence has not shifted substantially from its 1987 policy, stated in 'Confidential' Royal Navy documents, that, 'the potentially divisive influence of homosexual practices or other sexual deviations must be excluded ... Homosexual activities may also give rise to an unacceptable degree of doubt about an individual's fitness to have access to classified information.'

So, if homosexuality presents these risks, is divisive, warrants long-term expensive investigations and raises questions about security, an independent observer might turn to those countries where homosexuals do serve openly for evidence of these risks. But there is little evidence of any of the problems that the Ministry of Defence states that they would expect.

Most European armies are still largely conscripted and the British Ministry of Defence has said that for a conscription army to outlaw homosexuality would allow an easy way out for unwilling conscriptees. Putting aside the bizarre notion that large numbers of heterosexual men and women would want to brand themselves as homosexual malingerers for the rest of their lives in order to avoid a year's employment, the fact is that in many of the conscripting countries homosexuality already provides a route out, if the conscriptee wants to take it.

In France, for example, there is no ban on homosexuals serving, but if a gay man being called up for National Service does not wish to serve *because* of his homosexuality then alternative voluntary service arrangements can be made. In this situation the individual's homosexuality is treated in much the same way as conscientious objection. France, along with Denmark, Belgium, Italy and Finland says that only individuals whose homosexuality interferes with their ability effectively to perform their duties are to be discharged – but this can only happen after medical diagnoses have been provided, and the medical authorities have to state that individuals are unable to carry out their duties as a result of their sexuality; it is by no means automatic.

It is not a case of Europe alone being more liberal on this issue. In October 1992 Canada withdrew its ban on homosexuals serving after the Federal Court ruled that the ban was in violation of the Canadian Charter of Rights and Fundamental Freedoms. When the hearing took place the Department of National Defence did not attempt to defend the ban; the Department's Counsel said, 'We essentially decided we really didn't have any evidence to put in that would justify the policy.' For several years before this hearing the Department of National Defence had said that lesbians and gay men would not be sacked – but would not be promoted either – they were allowed to fulfil their periods of engagement and would not be re-enlisted. It was partly the successful service of individuals who were in this position which persuaded the Department to drop the ban completely.

The Canadian experience is not unique either; in the same year the New Zealand Parliament passed a general anti-discrimination law which encompassed sexual orientation. Although it was entitled to, the Defence Ministry did not apply for an exemption to this law. The result of this was that New Zealand's ban on lesbians and gay men serving in its Defence Force effectively ended in July 1992.

Canada and New Zealand both offer non-conscription models for the British Ministry of Defence to look to for evidence of the problems caused by homosexuals – but no evidence seems to exist. When I ask Susan Willett and Colonel Moorhouse at the Ministry to explain why they felt these countries offered no evidence of significant morale or disciplinary problems as a result of lifting their bans, Colonel Moorhouse pointed out what he said were the significant differences between the British armed forces and these countries' armed forces.

'The nature of our armed forces is different; for a variety of reasons we have one of the most professional forces in the world. We have a worldwide commitment that is only really matched by the Americans. Our forces do not spend a lot of time in one base with what are effectively nine-to-five jobs, they move around and live more closely with each other. We have the demands in Northern Ireland as well. For forces like the Australian one, where people spend many years in one place with a separate home life away from the camp the situation may be different, but in our armed forces the situation would be much more difficult.'

In general terms, Australia seem to offer Britain a close model for examination: our armed forces are very similar and work closely together regularly. The Australian Defence Force (the ADF) consists of nearly 65,000 men and women in three branches; the Royal Australian Navy, Royal Australian Air Force, and the Australian Army, and is a completely professional force. None of the states of Australia have any form of conscription or national service.

In structure, training, tradition and role the ADF is remarkably similar to the British armed forces. Driving past the Royal Australian Navy base in Sydney, past the line of moored grey destroyers and frigates flying the White Ensign you could be forgiven for thinking that you were in Portsmouth or Devonport. Wandering around the Royal Australian Air Force base in Perth, RAAF Pearce, amongst airmen wearing the same dull blue-grey uniforms, making derisive comments about flyers from foreign air forces borrowing their base, you could be forgiven for thinking that you were at RAF Kinloss or RAF Valley. The tall walls, built from an Australian form of Pennine gritstone, which surround Victoria Barracks in Sydney (overlooking the gay and lesbian Mardi Gras route) could have been designed by Palmerston to defend England's south coast from Napoleonic assault. The reality of the ADF today is that it is a highly trained professional defence force, investing heavily in new technologies and personnel to ensure that Australia's defence remains self-sufficient. The ADF is, however, smaller than the British armed forces, the total numbers in all three branches approximate to not much more than the manpower strength of the Royal Navy alone.

Australia sees its tropical, lightly populated northern flank as its most vulnerable, and much of the development of the ADF over the last few years has been directed at building this up – new airbases have been built to form a chain of five across the Northern Territories and Queensland, while mobile army units have been trained to work in this tough terrain, and a regular brigade is soon to be based in the north permanently. The navy is moving half its ships and all its new submarines to Perth on the west coast as part of its 'two-ocean strategy' – defence from the Indian Ocean and Pacific Ocean.

The navy has a fleet of 3 guided missile destroyers, 6 guided missile frigates, 3 destroyer escorts (which are very similar to Royal Navy Leander class frigates), 5 diesel-electric submarines, 15 patrol boats and 27 other ships. The Fleet Air Arm flies a range of helicopters and fixed-wing aircraft. Six ships from the Royal Australian Navy took part in the Gulf War.

The army is highly mobile, using Black-Hawk battlefield helicopters, light armoured vehicles, Leopard tanks, and armoured personnel carriers. A number of twin-rotor Chinook helicopters are being introduced as well. The army regularly carries out major exercises with the armed forces of other countries and participates in world 'peace-keeping' operations.

Australia also defends its interests with the air force's fleet of over 300 aircraft spearheaded by around 20 American-built F-111 strike aircraft, and 70 F/A-18 multi-role fighters. Both these types of aircraft can fire the Harpoon anti-ship missile and provide close air support for ground operations. About 20 P3 Orion long-range maritime reconnaissance aircraft provide an over-the-horizon anti-submarine and airborne early-warning capability, while a range of other aircraft provide transport, mid-air refuelling and patrol capabilities. One squadron flies visiting VIPs, including members of the royal family and senior members of the Government.

These are a modern professional army, navy and air force, any of whose members could instantly swap places with members of the British armed forces and do the same job.

For many years the ADF upheld a similar ban to the British on homosexuality, which is hardly surprising since the British wrote its original regulations. It is only relatively recently that the Australian Government has started to change the regulations in any appreciable way. No real counting has ever been done, but it seems reasonable to assume that several thousand people have lost their jobs, often dishonourably, for homosexuality, over the many years that the ban was in place.

In the late 1980s the issue of lesbian and gay rights began to edge its way on to the armed forces policy agenda, as well as into other areas like immigration. The first serious moves to see the ban lifted came when a number of individuals and groups within the Australian Labor Party tried to put the issue on to their Party's domestic agenda. After much internal debate, and a couple of small scandals in the ADF caused by overt sexual discrimination, a committee was formed to look at the issues of sexual behaviour in the ADF. A number of reasons for lifting the ban were presented to the Australian Labor Party Caucus Committee, which included the following: the ban was inherently discriminatory; any law that regulates or penalises homosexual activity impedes public health programmes promoting safer sex; the ban defied Australia's obligations under a number of international treaties, including the International Labor Organisation Charter 111; the continuation of the ban could be electorally damaging to the ALP; and continued witch-hunts threatened the dignity of ordinary Australians. The Labor Party machine was finally convinced and the Government began to talk about lifting the ban seriously in August 1992.

At the same time a Senate committee heard evidence from the ADF and others on this and other matters relating to sexual discrimination, and reported to the Cabinet in September 1992. As a result of this report, and after wider consultation, a decision was made to introduce a new policy on sexual conduct. The old policy stated: 'Homosexual behaviour is not accepted or condoned in the Defence Force.' Anyone admitting to, or proved to be involved in, homosexual behaviour was automatically sacked.

After all the committees and inquiries had reported, in November 1992 Prime Minister Paul Keating announced a new policy which ambiguously banned 'unacceptable sexual behaviour'.

Controversially, the Defence Minister, Robert Ray, initially told Parliament that unacceptable sexual behaviour would still include homosexual activity. However, at what highly placed sources suggest was a fairly raucous Cabinet meeting on 24 November 1992, Attorney-General Michael Duffy successfully argued that the discriminatory policy had to be dropped. It was. The new policy states that obscene behaviour, sexist language, unwelcome advances, requests for sexual favours and any assault are unacceptable in the Australian Defence Force and will be dealt with by disciplinary action. These rules apply equally to unwelcome heterosexual and homosexual behaviour.

The way in which the current policy is intended to work is best explained in the Defence Force's Guidance to Commanding Officers in the Annex entitled *Examples of Unacceptable Sexual Behaviour*:

> Any unwelcome sexual advance, unwelcome request for sexual favours or unwelcome conduct of a sexual nature is unacceptable sexual behaviour and warrants disciplinary or administrative action against the perpetrator ... Unwelcome sexual behaviour does not include action or conduct which reflects mutual respect, friendship or attraction.

Some examples of unwelcome sexual behaviour are:

a. spreading rumours regarding a colleague's sexual life;

b. public discussion of sexual activities – with the intention of embarrassing colleagues; and

c. derogatory remarks to a colleague regarding their sexual appeal.

Some other circumstances in which sexual behaviour would be unacceptable, together with the reasons for the unacceptability, include:

a. indiscreet sexual relationships between a superior and a subordinate, resulting in damage to unit cohesion and an undermining of the superior's authority;

b. public flaunting and the advocacy of a particular sexual proclivity, causing offence to members of the member's group and thus liable to provoke a breakdown in group cohesion and loss of professional respect; and

c. sexual relationships and activities conducted openly in the communal environment of a mess or barrack block, or encouraging younger members to accept participation in such activities as a requirement of communal living.

Consensual adult lesbian and gay relationships alone, it was decided, should no longer be grounds for sacking.

The story of how Paul Keating called the service chiefs into his office and told them of the decision has become part of Australian gay political folklore: he simply told them that there was a new policy and it was up to them to implement it. As soldiers, sailors and airmen, it was made clear, their job was to carry out orders, and this is what they did. A flurry of press comment greeted the decision, but the announcement was not followed by a mass 'coming out' of thousands of servicemen and women. Privately, however, a large number of men and women in the Australian Defence Force sighed with relief.

Royal Australian Air Force Sergeant David Mitchell is a communications specialist. He has been security cleared to a very high level and worked in particularly sensitive jobs and positions all over Australia. Until late 1993 he was also a secret homosexual. A sergeant's responsibilities in Australia often extend beyond those you would expect to see in the British armed forces.

'I used to lie about my life, although I'd given up lying more recently and just stopped talking about my private life at all. I'm the head of a department here, with several people working for me in the office, but I could not be honest with any of them about my sexuality before.

'Two years ago if my bosses had found out about my sexuality I would have lost my job, my pension benefits, my reputation. Now the Air Force are holding discrimination-awareness days that include sexuality as part of the talk. If somebody calls me faggot or worse, or actively discriminates against me I can make a complaint and it will be taken seriously.

'Until the change in the law I was a security risk – had somebody tried to blackmail me over my sexuality I would have been easy prey. I hope that I would have done the right thing, but the sense of belonging, of doing something worthwhile ... all the emotions that the armed forces encourage, that's a lot to say goodbye to if someone tries to blackmail you. It might be easier just to give them what they want, money or worse.

'So I used to lie about girlfriends. But there was always a major homoerotic undertone to a lot of life in the ADF, and strangely I think that was a lot harder for lesbians and gays to deal with – particularly those who hadn't yet come out. I remember in about 1980 I was in a lorry with a group of soldiers driving hundreds of miles for an exercise, and the guys kept wanking into a sandbag to pass the time. They'd come really loudly and then tell everyone that they had had a really good wank. I think one of them may have been cracking on to me, but I'm not really sure – I wasn't out to myself then. I, the gay man, was definitely the most uncomfortable with the situation.

'But even before I had come out to myself I used to speak out against homophobic comments. Maybe I was subconsciously dealing with the problem, but I always spoke up against discrimination.

145

'Now that lesbians and gays can serve openly in the ADF it doesn't mean that loads of dizzy queens are going to be coming out all over the place. The military is not the place for miles of fabulous pink chiffon.'

Sergeant Mitchell has been very lucky, he hasn't faced a problem with his colleagues at all since he came out. He took a birthday cake in recently for one of the women in his department. While the unit were eating the cake, his boss asked generally who had baked it. David didn't say anything, but one of the women said, 'Sergeant Mitchell's boyfriend, Peter.'

David had not discussed the subject of his sexuality with the boss, and was pleasantly surprised when he turned and said, 'Will you tell him it's a very good cake.'

David 'came out' officially while he was in England. He was serving with the RAF on an exchange programme, and living in a Sergeants' Mess alongside British airmen. This was in the summer of 1993, and he had not yet declared his homosexuality at his home base near Perth – but he was aware that he could. The situation in Britain annoyed him, and he went public, so that his Government and his British colleagues would know that he was gay.

'I was allowed to be openly gay, and if anything had happened my Government would have backed me up. But if one of my British colleagues had come with me to a gay bar or night club he would have risked losing his job.'

Amongst NATO member countries only Turkey, Italy and the USA, along with Britain, still outlaw homosexuality, and so, in this age of combined 'peace-keeping' and 'United Nations Police' operations like the Desert Storm in the Gulf, Yugoslavia or Rwanda, a situation of this kind must arise time and again – an 'out' gay man or lesbian serving alongside colleagues from forces where their sexuality would be outlawed.

The Ministry of Defence says that it has issued no guidelines for members of the British armed forces who find themselves serving with forces which do not outlaw homosexuality. If it really believes that the 'potentially divisive

146

influence of homosexual practices' or other 'sexual deviations' must be excluded, then it seems logical to expect the Ministry of Defence to have prepared for this eventuality and issued guidance.

The Australian experience has not been completely smooth. David Mitchell says: 'I would be a fool to say that there will not be problems, or that there aren't many in the ADF who think lifting the ban is wrong, but the Senate Inquiry into Sexual Harassment has been very public, and as a result, everyone in the ADF knows that making abusive comments to me about my sexuality is no different from making rude comments about Aboriginals.

'I was, and still am a good sergeant – people can't just change their opinions of me because they find out that I'm gay. At the time of the debate on the subject in the autumn of 1992, I found that colleagues in their thirties and forties were most understanding. It was younger guys that seemed to have more of a problem. Now they know, colleagues with sons still want me to babysit.'

But, as Sergeant Mitchell says, there are areas of the ADF that seem to be encountering more difficulties than others. Army bases and air force stations seem to have the least problems, and the Royal Australian Navy the most.

Able Seaman David Goodwin joined the RAN when he was eighteen in 1991. He knew he was gay when he joined, but hadn't yet 'come out'.

'I had never had sex with a man before I joined, but I had no girlfriend either, I always brushed off questions about girlfriends. Being gay was still illegal then and I knew it was a problem – there were stories about people being thrown out during training, although I didn't know any of them.

'It's really hard to come out, you're living with a secret – where have you been at weekends? I invented girlfriends, changed the names of the guys I'd seen to girls' names so that I could talk about them without a problem. I used phrases like "my partner" to get around the problem. I found life really difficult and felt alone all the time. I told two girls on the ship, and they were really positive. But the reality is that life would be impossible for me if I came out properly.

'One girl on the ship, she's a lesbian and she was very open about it. She had big problems. It was the guys, not the girls that harassed her. It was like they couldn't cope with the idea that she wasn't available. But she eventually tried the ADF freephone number to report sexual harassment. Ultimately the only way that the ADF would take action is if she named the people that were harassing her. That's a really stupid idea because if she dropped other people in the shit who would want to serve alongside her in the future? She left the navy instead.

'Some people on my ship have suspected that I'm gay. It's difficult to keep it secret for long. I never had a visible girlfriend. The comments are funny at first, but they really get you down quite hard after a while. Guys drop the soap when you're in the shower and dare each other to bend over and pick it up. I became socially very isolated when they started to suspect me. The stress stared to affect me quite hard and I spoke to a psychologist and a law enforcement officer, but I didn't tell them I was gay and they said that they could only take action against people if I named names.'

The hierarchy in the ADF has responded to the new situation much more quickly than the grass roots, although videos on sexual harassment have now been shown throughout the ADF at all levels. Colonel Moorhouse at the British Ministry of Defence says that as the Australians tend to spend longer at one base and don't keep moving around in tight-knit groups they may find things easier – but Australia is an enormous country and most of the bases are pretty remote. Colonel Moorhouse is right that families in Britain may be physically protected and shut off from the outside world by fences around married quarters and by accommodation blocks, as a result of IRA terrorism, but the outside world is just on the other side of a gate; in Australia many of the accommodation areas or estates of private housing near bases may not be fenced in, but they might as well be since they are surrounded by miles of empty scrub. Even Sergeant Mitchell's base which is 'local' to Perth is an hour's drive from the city through remote countryside, sparsely populated and filled with exotic rural wildlife, black cockatoos, kangaroos and snakes. If Colonel Moorhouse thinks 'popping out' to be gay is easier there than Army Headquarters at Wilton or on Salisbury Plain, then I think he is mistaken. The landscape may be more dramatic and the wildlife more intriguing, but the military community is no less insular. And there are no wild black cockatoos on Salisbury Plain.

The new Australian policy does not specifically outlaw sexual relationships, homosexual or heterosexual, between serving members of the Defence Force, provided that they fall into the new category of 'acceptable sexual behaviour'. Provided that the relationship is consensual and does not constitute obscene behaviour it will not automatically be viewed as 'unacceptable'.

Able Seaman Darren Goodes has had one relationship with a fellow sailor and says that this did not cause many problems.

'We conducted the relationship off-base, and away from the ship. We were quite sensible about it. It is true that it can be difficult to leave any problems in the relationship at home, and maybe having a relationship with someone in the same unit is a bad idea. But that applies to straights too.'

The environment within the Royal Australian Navy is not yet positive enough for Darren Goodes to feel able to come out at work. In fact so far there has been so little difference in the climate aboard ships that he is intending to leave the navy instead.

'If I was to stay in and "come out" I'd always be watching my back. Some positive role models might help but unlike the army or the air force no one is yet being visible in the navy. My ship has a complement of a hundred and forty, and I am aware of five other homosexuals serving on board. Of those two have been removed, one to another base and another from the navy altogether. One other has resigned. Now I'm going too.'

The problem seems to be that the only way for lesbians and gays to ask for help is to call in the big guns from the Department of Defence anti-harassment department and risk their reputations even further by naming those who they believe are guilty of discrimination. What David Goodwin seems to be suggesting is that each unit needs its own anti-harassment officer, who can take action in a more general, less formal and less disciplinary manner.

The new guidelines mention a network of sexual harassment contact officers, but the experience of the men and women I spoke to was that this system has yet to prove itself on a local level. The procedure is fine in principle for serious cases of sexual harassment, but for the more run-of-the-mill situations the new guidelines allow for more junior supervisors to react directly to a complaint.

'Depending on their judgement of the gravity of a case, supervisors should first try to achieve resolution informally. The objective should always be a situation where the undesirable behaviour not only ceases but is not repeated.'

In the Royal Australian Navy at least, for lesbians and gay men, this informal route to resolution is taking a while to sort out.

Eileen, an army lieutenant in Sydney who works in administration and personnel, since the ban was lifted has come out to close friends and colleagues, but she is not confident that 'coming out' officially would not prejudice her reports and chances of promotion.

'I guess I'm still in the closet really at work, but when I go out now to a bar or a club I'm not worrying about being seen when I leave. It's not a risk now, it would be just embarrassing.'

Opponents of change talk about the special conditions pertaining to military service, and the damage that homosexuals could cause to the morale and discipline of units under great stress in times of war. It is clearly the case that there are enormous areas of potential stress in the armed forces. Working under fire or the threat of it, in close proximity to colleagues often for long periods of time, in a ship or infantry unit, places an enormous burden on the inter-personal relationships that exist within that unit.

Many of those opposed to change, the British Ministry of

Defence in particular, but also a number of vocal Members of Parliament, believe very strongly that the presence of lesbians and gay men within those units would have a substantial detrimental effect on discipline and morale. This, however, is not the experience of lesbian and gay members of the Dutch armed forces who have served recently in a number of dangerous locations.

Joost Shaberg, Vice-President of the Foundation for Homosexuals in the Forces in the Netherlands, says, 'In the last three months three of our board have gone to serve in Bosnia, and another member of the group has gone to Rwanda/Zaire. It is not necessary for them to be secretive about their sexuality. In fact it is our experience that it is easier for people if they are open about it.'

As part of the personnel training for officers in the Dutch Armed Forces, courses on discrimination in the workplace and sexuality are held – and the experience of those teaching them is that the initial level of homophobia or misunderstanding of homosexuals is no lower than one would expect it to be in the United Kingdom. It is a figment of the British media's collective imagination that the Netherlands has an inherently liberal attitude towards sexual matters.

The Netherlands is a surprisingly religious small country which, for example, expects high moral standards from its children and in its education system. The armed forces, when viewed alongside the rest of Dutch society, are fairly reactionary and conservative, and the initial reaction of many of the officers and others attending the courses on discrimination and homosexuality has been negative. However, the officers who run them say that it is surprising just how easily and quickly people change their minds once they have an opportunity to discuss the issues in a positive environment – talking about the facts not the rumours.

There are cultural differences between NATO member countries which affect the nature of their military attitude to homosexuality. Italy, for example, which has a theoretical ban on homosexuality, has a cultural attitude to sexuality which has resulted in a pragmatic approach to the enforcement of their ban: Italians tend to think of homosexuality as

151

an act rather than a condition, and so treat homosexual behaviour between members of the armed forces as a disciplinary offence. For the most part homosexuality is not treated as an important issue, and the 'witch-hunts' which are so familiar here are not instigated. British forces work closely with the Italian armed forces on a regular basis. At the time of writing British RAF and Royal Navy aircraft are using bases in Italy, for example, in order to help police the 'no-fly zone' over Bosnia.

Filippo Cernetti did his Italian National Service in the army in 1989. During the three-day interview and assessment which all recruits attend he was asked if he was homosexual. He said he wasn't. 'Why would anyone say they were gay? It is true that they would not have to do the National Service, but their police records would say that they were gay for the rest of their lives.'

There is a definition used by sociologists: MSM (men who have sex with men). These use this definition, rather than 'gay' because many of the men who have sex with other men do not acknowledge themselves to be gay. In Italy this definition is particularly useful as many of Filippo's colleagues in the army were men who would always assert their heterosexuality, and would eventually get married and have children, while also continuing to have occasional sexual contact with men. A public declaration of homosexuality is less common in southern Europe than in some northern European countries. So there are many members of the Italian armed forces who appear to be heterosexual, but who also regularly engage in homosexual activity. The definitions are blurred in the same way that they are for many bisexual members of the British armed forces. Filippo Cernetti believes that this is what an observer of Italian culture would expect.

'People don't talk about being gay. It fits in with Italian culture. I had sex with several other soldiers – including one "straight" guy in Piacera where we pushed our beds together and he enjoyed the thrill for a while. When he said he didn't want to play any more we just stopped. I also had very exciting sex with an NCO who was very nervous about being thought of as gay.

'After a while I decided not to involve myself sexually with other soldiers who were not prepared to acknowledge that they were gay. If you are gay then you can easily become an available sex toy for "straight" soldiers – I was interested in finding a relationship.'

If homosexual activity does come to the attention of the Italian military authorities then they will take action to stop it. This *can* include dismissal, but other disciplinary measures are open to the authorities, and it is by no means certain that an individual will be sacked.

Other countries manage to introduce a range of policies and disciplinary guidelines that allow for measures to be taken that can deal with this kind of 'unacceptable sexual behaviour'. Australia, with its straightforward guidelines provides the best model for the way that Britain could move. With a social framework and military structures that are strikingly familiar it is difficult for anyone to argue convincingly that a policy which is beginning to work in Australia would fail decisively here. A policy along the lines of the Australian code would also encourage men and women dismissed for their sexuality not to take the British Government to court. Failure to introduce new policies will only reinforce these individuals' determination to pursue litigation, and Britain could easily end up following the American model, where there are about 130 cases before the courts.

10

DON'T ASK – DON'T TELL

PRESIDENT BILL CLINTON was elected in November 1992 with the fullest possible support of the lesbian and gay political community in the United States. No presidential candidate has ever so deliberately and successfully courted the lesbian and gay vote, and an estimated 3.5 million dollars were contributed to his campaign by the lesbian and gay community. In a speech to lesbian and gay community leaders in Los Angeles Bill Clinton said, 'I have a vision and you are part of it.'

On the night of the election, the gay bars and clubs around DuPont Circle in Washington DC were packed with the generally conservative lawyers, lobbyists and members of the US armed forces who make up a large proportion of Washington's gay population. And although many of them were traditionally Republican voters, they were all celebrating the Democratic victory.

A pro-gay President had been elected, a man who had openly employed a number of lesbians and gay men as senior figures in his election campaign. Most importantly of all, the promise to lift the ban on homosexuals in the US military was going to become a reality, so for many of the customers that night, who work by day at the Pentagon and the other military establishments that encircle the nation's capital, there really was something to celebrate.

During the next couple of months, as the nascent Administration prepared itself for 20 January 1993 and Bill Clinton's inauguration, many lesbians and gays in the US Military felt enormous relief. As the media storm on the 'Gays in the Military' issue worked itself up into a fully fledged hurricane, a number of serving lesbians and gays felt secure enough with the new Administration's stated policy to 'come out'.

Four days after the presidential election, Navy Petty Officer Phillips, a nuclear-reactor technician revealed his sexual orientation to his supervisor.

Lieutenant Zoë Dunning, a 1985 Naval Academy graduate and Stanford MBA came out at a rally in support of President Clinton on 16 January 1993.

On 29 January 1993 Marine Sergeant Justin Elzie, who is rated in the top 10 per cent of all US Marines, came out on an evening news show.

Navy Lieutenant Tracy Thorne came out on American television show, *Nightline*, in May 1993.

Men and women in all branches of the American armed forces took their new commander-in-chief at his word, and told colleagues and bosses that they were gay.

Unfortunately, they came out just a little too quickly. Right-wing political energy was being channelled into preventing President Clinton from carrying out his promise. The White House suffered a telephone 'meltdown' as up to 68,000 calls a day were logged from individuals wanting to register their disapproval. The chairman of the Joint Chiefs of Staff, General Colin Powell – riding high on rumours that he was about to embark on a political career himself – made his opposition to lifting the ban clear. Questions were raised about the appropriateness of a serving officer questioning so publicly the intended actions of his commander-in-chief – but the Defense Department cited the Goldwater-Nichols Act in its defence, in which the obligations of the chairman of the Joint chiefs as the President's primary military adviser are outlined. The Defense Department said that in opposing the ban General Powell was fulfilling his obligations as the President's adviser. General Powell was successful. President Clinton backed down and instituted his notorious 'Don't ask – Don't tell' policy. After months of policy argument, all those men and women who came out are now in the process of being sacked. Navy Petty Officer Phillips was processed for an honourable discharge after the new policy was announced, and is now suing the Defense Department in an attempt to keep his job. Lieutenant Zoë Dunning was immediately recommended for discharge by her commanding officer, who also manipulated her duty assignments and performance evaluations. Through legal protest she was able to correct the evaluations, but this did not stop her being recommended for discharge on 10 June 1993. The theoretically independent Discharge Board was apparently ordered to come to the conclusion that she should be dismissed by her base commander, Admiral Ruck. Lieutenant Dunning is now waiting on a Defense Department investigation into the alleged 'improper command influence' exercised by him. Lieutenant Tracy Thorne is suing the Defense Department over his dismissal as well.

Sergeant Justin Elzie, who has had highly prestigious postings as a US embassy guard, was recommended for an honourable discharge at a board held on 31 March 1993. In its recommendations the board described Justin Elzie as an 'exemplary Marine'. On 1 September 1993 Sergeant Elzie received orders that placed him in the Stand-by Reserve. Following legal arguments he was reinstated to active duty; but shortly afterwards the US Supreme Court made an interim ruling on another case which gave the Defense Department further reason to believe that it will ultimately win the outstanding cases. Based on its belief that the discharges will be upheld, Sergeant Elzie was removed from active duty again. In response he went to the federal courts himself and won the right to be reinstated to active duty yet again while the case between him and the Defense Department continues. The determination by the Defense Department to fight each case tooth and nail seems to fly in the face of the 'positive' approach to lesbian and gay service men and women which Bill Clinton had used to such good electoral effect in his presidential campaign a year before.

The new 'Don't ask – Don't tell' policy was introduced in June 1993 and states that applicants will no longer be asked if they are lesbian or gay on entry to the armed forces, but will be told what is and what is not acceptable behaviour. Homosexual behaviour is not acceptable.

The policy is a mis-match of contradictory statements and ambiguities. It states, for examples, that homosexual orientation will not in itself be a bar to service unless it is 'manifested by homosexual conduct'. To most normal observers 'homosexual conduct' can only be distinguished by some form of homosexual sexual activity, but according to the policy any acknowledgement that a man or woman is gay counts as 'homosexual conduct'. The act of saying 'I'm gay', even if the individual is not involved in any form of sexual activity, is viewed as homosexual conduct, and will result in dismissal – despite the fact that the policy states that 'sexual orientation will not be a bar to service'.

The new policy states that the US Military will discharge any individual who engages in homosexual conduct, which includes making a statement that they are homosexual or bisexual, or anyone who marries, or attempts to marry someone of the same gender.

The policy also states that no investigations will be carried out solely to determine a service member's sexual orientation. This is an attempt to prevent the 'witch-hunts' that have provided such powerful stories for the media over the last ten years. Commanders will initiate inquiries only where there is 'credible information' that a basis for discharge or disciplinary action exists. This statement is complete nonsense, because 'homosexual conduct' of any sort *is* a 'basis for discharge' and so effectively commanders can initiate inquiries at will. One of the biggest criticisms of the new policy is the degree of latitude allowed to individual commanders in deciding how to enforce the new policy. Liberal and sympathetic commanders can legitimately ignore allegations on the basis that they do not constitute 'credible information', while their less broad-minded colleagues can investigate every possible avenue, citing the same regulation as their basis for action.

Some attempt has been made to outline what constitutes 'credible information'. For example an allegation or statement by one service member that another service member is a homosexual is not by itself grounds for either a criminal investigation or a Commander's inquiry. However there have been a number of cases where the US Marines in particular seem to have ignored this regulation and initiated investigations because of allegations of precisely this nature.

The new policy also states: 'Bodily contact between service members of the same sex of a type generally considered as homosexual, such as hand-holding or kissing, in most circumstances will be sufficient to initiate separation.'

But while the policy says that holding hands is grounds for sacking it goes on to say that association with known homosexuals, presence at a gay bar, possessing or reading homosexual publications or marching in a gay rights rally in civilian clothes will not by themselves be enough to initiate an investigation.

The policy also makes it clear that anything stated in confidence to a priest, husband or wife, or lawyer, remains confidential. This does not extend to discussions with a doctor, and one US serviceman is losing his job after he confided in a service doctor.

According to interested legal and service veterans' groups, the ambiguities in the policy and the leeway given to commanding officers, allow the policy *in action* to remain pretty much the same as it was before. As these groups point out, men and women can still be discharged simply for saying that they are gay – no 'homosexual conduct' has to have taken place. Gay and lesbian personnel can still be jailed for up to fifteen years for the same acts permitted to heterosexuals – including holding hands, kissing and 'adult sexual activity', even if the conduct is consensual and takes place off duty, off-base and in private.

Commanders and investigators may still seize and examine personal diaries and letters for evidence, and medical officers still have no duty of confidentiality to their patients. In an investigation and at a subsequent discharge board an accused serviceman or woman cannot object to the entering of any evidence even if it was obtained through coercion, threats or harassment.

Colonel Margarethe Cammermeyer, described by *Newsweek* magazine as a 'walking recruiting poster', joined the US army in the 1960s and served in Vietnam where she supervised a hospital for wounded and dying soldiers, and among many decorations was awarded the Bronze Star. She had risen to become chief nurse of the Washington National Guard when she was asked a question about her sexuality during a routine investigation required for a higher level of security clearance for a promotion in July 1991 – after twenty-six years' service. The army discharged her as soon as it could, but in 1994 she was reinstated after taking the case to court. This relief may be only temporary, however, and Colonel Cammermeyer continues to wait for federal courts, and ultimately the US Supreme Court, to decide finally whether or not the bans on lesbians and gays is constitutional. In Britain we have no written constitution to appeal to – which, whilst reducing the volume of work (and fees) for lawyers fighting the ban in Britain, means that dismissed British servicemen and women have to look to the European courts for remedy. This is a process no more certain – and certainly no quicker – than appealing to the US Supreme Court.

Many of the American cases are 'on hold' as federal judges await the outcome of the case of Petty Officer Keith Meinhold, who was discharged from the navy for admitting he was gay on national television in May 1992. He immediately challenged the legality of his discharge, arguing that the ban was unconstitutional. In early 1993 the district court for the Central District of California agreed with his argument and found no rational or legitimate basis for the policy – and, alarmingly for the Defense Department, issued an injunction against all dismissals for homosexuality.

Of course, the 'pro-gay' Clinton Administration challenged this decision in the Appeal courts, and the case of Meinhold *v.* United States Department of Defense, as it is batted to and fro on its way to the Supreme Court, continues to lead the legal challenge to the ban.

While the legal challenges continue, commanding officers in the United States are not slowing down their investigations into homosexuality. The Marines in particular seem unwilling to change their tough anti-gay stance.

In June 1994 Sergeant Robert Nadel was told that he would be court-martialled for committing homosexual acts. Sergeant Nadel was questioned on two occasions after the new policy came into effect at his base camp at Camp Hansen on the Pacific island of Okinawa. He was asked if he had had sex with a male friend. He denied that he had and was released. Three days later he was interviewed again and this time the interrogation was much tougher. He was told he was lying, and asked if he had touched the crotch of another Marine without his consent. Sergeant Nadel, who was by now very scared, admitted that he had touched the other Marine, but he said that the other man had come on to him. He believes that the investigators had forced the other Marine to make the allegations or face charges that he was gay himself. By doing this the investigators ensure that they have 'credible information' that an offence has been committed. This tactic has been used with considerable success in Britain as well. After the interrogation Sergeant Nadel's room was searched and his friends were brought in for questioning.

This seems to have been one of a number of related investigations at Camp Hansen in Okinawa, where over 20,000 US Marines are stationed. The Service Members' Legal Defense Network in Washington DC says that it has reports of investigators in Okinawa routinely asking soldiers to name others they believe to be gay, again directly in contravention of the new 'Don't ask – Don't tell' policy.

The US Marines have also been using details of consultations between patient and doctor to initiate investigations into alleged homosexuality. Corporal Kevin Blaesing went to see the base psychologist at the naval hospital in Charleston, South Carolina, to ask what he thought were confidential questions about his sexual orientation. The report that the psychologist subsequently wrote found Corporal Blaesing 'fit for full duty', but the Commander concluded from the medical report that he was homosexual.

The psychologist had suggested to Corporal Blaesing that

he might find things easier if he applied for a discharge, but when Blaesing decided that he wished to continue his career, he was told that he would be discharged 'by reason of homosexual admission', in June 1994.

For those men and women who have not come out, their position under the Clinton compromise is not dissimilar to that of their British counterparts. Kevin is a US Navy nuclear engineering officer, who has not come out at work.

'I guess I knew I was gay from when I was about eleven after watching a TV show about it – I kind of thought I was like that. But I didn't like it or want to be like that at all. I knew the Air Force Academy at Colorado Springs and I thought that if I joined the forces and wore a uniform like that then the girls would find me attractive and I wouldn't be gay any more.

'I went to Annapolis and had a few dates with girls, but I knew that they weren't right, but I started seeing a Mormon girl regularly because that was safe – there was no question of sex before marriage – she was strict about religion, and that made things easier. Intimacy scared me with a woman, and I didn't kiss her more than I would my sister. She followed me to Idaho and to Orlando when I had to move on for nuclear engineering training. We kept on dating, and she said that she was ready to get married – but I still had this big issue to resolve before I could get married – I still hadn't dealt with the gay thing.'

Kevin's career progressed. He qualified and began serving on board a nuclear attack submarine based on the west coast of the United States and in Hawaii. He was still trying to work out if he was really gay. Inevitably though, as seems to happen with so many men and women even in the most negative of environments, if they are homosexual, one way or another it's going to surface.

'I was at a video store while we were at Pearl Harbor looking at the gay videos, and a guy gave me his card. I called him later and we met and went back to his place. I didn't tell him my surname or unit or anything, but I spent a few nights there and of course people noticed how upbeat I was at work and they thought I was with a girl.

'It was in April 1992 that I went to Los Angeles and really "came out". I met guys and had sexual relationships with them. Then my cousin took me to a bar in Honolulu and I met an enlisted man from the boat who was "out" too. Nothing happened between us, but I found the risks worrying. By August 1993 I was aware of five other gay people on our boat who were "out" to themselves.'

Kevin has never felt able to be completely open, even with his gay colleagues, because the risks are too great.

'After I broke up with the last guy I was seeing I went back to the ship and one of my bags that went to the laundry had a gay magazine in it. That evening my boss called me and said they had found the magazine. I just played dumb and said that I knew nothing about it. He treated me oddly for a while, but once I started making "straight" comments our relationship returned to normal. Once when we were in Brisbane one of the other gay guys on board came on to me really strongly and wanted to leave the bar with me. I had to stop the situation because it would not be right to get involved with someone from the ship.'

Kevin has now served ten years as an officer in the US Navy. Although a very highly trained nuclear engineering officer, he is probably going to leave in the next year because he does not want to risk his career ending in ruins. The new policy does not seem to have stopped this haemorrhage of talent, as American service people, just like their British colleagues, decide to get out while the going is good.

Michelle Benecke is one of the directors of the Service Members' Legal Defense Network, based in Washington DC, which provides emergency legal services to men and women in the military hurt by the gay ban, monitors the implementation of the new policy and takes a pro-active approach to dealing with abuses of power and cases of harassment during military investigations. The group produces professional policy analyses for the Administration and for Congress, and uses these to try to accelerate the overthrow of the ban.

The group has had a number of significant successes as its professional legal approach to countering the problems men and women are experiencing gathers momentum. Its strategy has so far stopped a number of 'witch-hunts' just as they were getting going; persuaded a number of commanding officers to drop court-martial charges; and linked together the 130 men and women who are taking the Defense Department to court over their dismissals. The organisation has also helped a number of men and women to ensure that their discharge is honourable in situations where the military establishment has often pushed for harsher penalties.

Michelle Benecke was an army captain and battery commander. Subsequently she has become a leading spokeswoman on the ban and in particular on its effect on women. She qualified in law at Harvard and at the University of Virginia, and set up the Service Members' Legal Defense Network with fellow lawyer C. Dixon Osburn as a result of the new Clinton policy. The group has been an immediate success.

Michelle Benecke explains: 'In the last eight months we have had over two hundred calls for help from men and women who have been caught or who are suspected of being gay. We are the only group that is properly monitoring the way that the new policy works in action. As we are Washington-based we have become a serious part of the debate on the issue here and try to keep up to date on all that is being said or thought.

'The White House now want to be seen as entirely separate from this issue – calls to it on the subject are referred to the Defense Department. We have heard from a very highly placed source at the Department that this issue was dropped by the Clinton Administration in return for the Pentagon's help in the defense review and cuts. The issue was used as a bargaining chip.

'The Pentagon is digging in its heels, but many now feel that change is inevitable – including a significant number of serving officers. The Clinton dallying caused confusion. The number of investigations was definitely stepped up as a result.

But there appears to be a new defiance and willingness to fight by individuals. They want to fight back. According to the Service Members' Legal Defense Network the anti-gay attitude in the forces has become more noticeable too, as everyone starts making anti-gay comments in order to assert their "straightness".'

In Britain the equivalent group, Rank Outsiders, has up until now been refused permission to run advertisements in the navy, army, and air force newspapers and magazines. But the Service Members' Legal Defense Network has not encountered the same difficulties: 'We have run adverts in the papers three times driving home the message that people should not be pressured into making a statement, and that they should always seek legal advice and representation. In a sense we try and offer a legal buffer.'

The success of the approach has resulted in some effusive letters of thanks from those affected. The following, signed 'A Grateful Naval Officer' shows how the approach works for people:

> I was initially facing a court martial for an alleged homosexual act – dancing with and embracing another man while intoxicated. This was subsequently deemed worthy of an administrative discharge without even a hearing. The military lawyer I was working with was quite capable, however he did not possess the power or the necessary clout to successfully argue my case to the Navy. By getting civilian counsel involved, the Navy was required to take a closer look and could not summarily process my case as they too often do. The Service Members' Legal Defense Network was the means of obtaining such qualified counsel with interests in seeing justice done.
>
> Due to the hard work and dedication of outside counsel, I successfully argued against separation. I would like to extend my heartfelt thanks to the Service Members' Legal Defense Network for giving me the opportunity to continue my career as a naval aviator.

Michelle Benecke is optimistic that the Supreme Court will support the view that the ban is unconstitutional. But even if it supports the doctrine of military deference – which since

1948 has given way to the military's stated requirement to limit an individual's liberty and personal rights in order to maintain an effective military machine – the legal challenge will be far from over: 'As the current cases that have got a long way in the legal process are dismissals under the old policy, there will be another group under the new policy which should get to the Supreme Court in three or four years. I can't believe that the US Supreme Court could easily support the "Don't ask – Don't tell" policy which is intrinsically flawed.'

For Britain, which is considerably less liberal than the United States in its approach to homosexual servicemen and women – still officially sanctioning 'witch-hunts' and commending servicemen and women for reporting their suspicions about their colleagues – the Clinton compromise does not offer a useful way forward.

II

THE ROAD TO CHANGE

HOWEVER DIFFICULT LIFE may be for lesbians and gay men in Britain's armed forces, the *status quo* is not going to change by itself. Rapid social change is anathema to the conservative British civil service and the political system. The officials and senior officers at the Ministry of Defence will not change policy for its own sake. Even if the Ministry of Defence was convinced by the arguments that the ban was unnecessary and expensive – motivation and energy from outside would still be necessary to make the MOD lift it.

If we exclude the unlikely possibility that Ministry officials along with admirals, general and air commodores will jointly press the Government to lift the ban themselves, then we are left with two possible routes to change. The political route requires that Members of Parliament become convinced the ban should be lifted and persuade the Government of the day to do so; while the judicial route requires men and women who have been dismissed to challenge the legality of their sacking in the British and European courts.

Both of these routes involve a level of organisation and activism that has not existed before amongst dismissed servicemen and women. The naturally conservative attitude and background of most former members of the armed forces has probably been the reason why it has taken such a long time for a politically motivated group to form to challenge the current policy. The group Rank Outsiders was only founded in 1991, but its reputation and effectiveness have grown over its first three years with startling speed.

The group was started by Army Lieutenant Elaine Chambers and Army Warrant Officer Robert Ely as a result of a House of Commons Select Committee inquiry into the subject in 1991. Robert's own story was listened to in detail by the committee, and is familiar.

'I joined the army on my seventeenth birthday – I was not from a rich family and so there was no chance for me to stay on at school, we couldn't have afforded it. That was in 1966. It is really quite stupid to ask me if I knew that I was gay then as the word didn't even exist – not for me anyway. Remember, the law didn't change until 1967, so it wasn't possible to be gay anywhere in British life then. I had always wanted to go into the band world, but initially joined the Royal Signals. While I was an apprentice I played the organ every Sunday, and the chaplain spoke to the director of music who recommended that I be transferred to the band. I trained for a year at the army's music school and became a full-time clarinettist with the Royal Corps of Signals Band. I then learned to play the flute as well, and started to play that in the band instead. I visited Cyprus and Germany playing with the Signals' Band.

'In 1972 I transferred to the Household Cavalry, the Life Guards, and learned to ride, as I was joining a mounted band. I played the piccolo on horseback. In 1976 I was selected to train as a band master and went off to the music school again to train. In 1979, as a warrant officer first class, I was transferred to the 2nd Battalion, the Parachute Regiment where I stayed until 1986. I served in Northern Ireland for two years, in Belize in South America and in Kenya. In 1983 the band went to Jamaica, and we represented Britain at the national independence anniversary celebrations. In 1984 the structure of the bands was changed and I moved to Bulford Camp to take over one of the new bands.'

Throughout his army career Robert never visited a gay bar or night club. He occasionally met men in 'cruising areas': car parks, areas of woodland and other similar places. In the 1970s Robert got married, but it only lasted a year.

'We got on very well, but I couldn't cope with being in the bedroom with her. That was the problem – I couldn't bear sharing the bed. After we got divorced things got easier in some ways as when colleagues asked about my relationships I could just say I was divorced. That answered most questions.'

Robert bought a house in a village near his new base, and to help pay the costs took in a lodger, a student who subsequently turned out to be gay. By another coincidence the student was also involved in a relationship with another bandsman, who was based in Germany. Robert and his lodger's bandsman boyfriend exchanged a couple of letters, and these were the eventual cause of his dismissal.

'On 7 June 1986, a Saturday, at 9.15 in the morning the SIB came to my front door and announced, "We have reason to believe you have been involved in homosexuality." I was still in my dressing gown and asked if I could go upstairs and shave and dress, which they allowed me to do. When I came down I said that the allegation was probably true and asked what would happen next. They were very polite and professional – probably because I was a warrant officer and they were sergeants. They said that they were going to search my house, which they did. They looked at everything, right the way through my house, from top to bottom, and took quite a few things away with them. They took my address book and letters. We then went to the SIB offices and I was interrogated all day. I was asked if I wanted a lawyer or a colleague present – but I was so embarrassed about it all that I said no. They suggested that I spoke to a lawyer, and phoned one that they knew for me. I spoke to him and his advice was to tell them whatever they wanted to know – no wonder they wanted me to speak to him.'

Robert talked honestly and openly about everything that had happened to him, and was then taken to see the officer of the day at his home. The officer was sympathetic and said, 'This must be devastating for you.' However, he also explained to Robert that he was to be held *incommunicado* in the Mess while the SIB checked through all the names in his diary and address book.

'My real concern was my dog, Rags, who was at home, and had been all day without being fed. I was taken back home to collect Rags and then held in the Mess waiting to hear what was going to happen. I had to eat in my room to start with so that I wouldn't talk to other people – that lasted about four days – and I seriously contemplated killing myself for the first time in my life. I was about to cut my wrists with a knife when Rags jumped up on the bed and looked at me. I didn't kill myself for the sake of my dog. I had no real friends outside the service at all, and after almost twenty years my whole life was in the process of collapsing around me.'

Four years later, in 1990, former Band Master Robert Ely was living in Bristol, effectively unemployed, surviving on occasional periods of temporary work. He went to a meeting of a local gay group and while there picked up a leaflet from Stonewall, the British political lobbying group for lesbian and gay equality. Robert was impressed by the sense that the group seemed to show in its approach to various issues – and wrote – enclosing £5 and explaining what had happened to him. Stonewall was aware that the issue was going to be raised in the House of Commons Armed Forces Bill Select Committee meetings in 1991, so wrote back asking Robert to write down his whole story.

'Then the phone rang one evening, and it was Stonewall asking me to come up to London the next day to give evidence at the committee myself. Of course I went, but I was absolutely terrified. I was shaking inside. Finally someone was going to listen to my story.

'After the committee hearing I put a letter in the *Pink Paper* [the national newspaper for lesbians and gay men based in London] asking if anyone else wanted to get in touch so that I could compile a number of case histories. The day that the letter was run, Elaine Chambers phoned me and we spoke for two hours. I had never spoken to anyone else that had been through it themselves before. We set up the group, Rank Outsiders, shortly afterwards to provide support to others in the same position.'

In 1994 the Ministry of Defence met Rank Outsiders and Stonewall for the first time to discuss 'welfare issues' and subsequently agreed to pass the phone number of the Rank

Outsiders' helpline to all units, so that it could be given to men and women facing investigation and dismissal. But providing better understanding and support to those who are being sacked is only part of the story. These groups, and the many individuals affected by the current policy, intend to see the policy lifted, not just implemented more humanely.

The Ministry of Defence is looking increasingly isolated in its view that homosexuality is 'incompatible' with military service. As we have seen, lesbians and gay men work in responsible jobs for many months after they have 'come out', whilst awaiting their dismissal. The Ministry clearly does not believe that homosexuals are completely incapable of working in a military environment: not if it continues to give them loaded automatic assault rifles and expects them to form guard patrols in the London suburbs like RAF Corporal Ian Waterhouse; not if it expects them to take on secret policy jobs at underground bunkers like Lieutenant-Commander Duncan Lustig-Prean; not if it expects them to continue as the nursing officer in sole charge of a busy hospital like Lieutenant Elaine Chambers.

The shibboleth, 'homosexuality is incompatible with military service', is beginning to look very shaky. This is a doctrine which costs the tax payer between £10 million and £20 million a year to uphold, and perhaps partly because of this there is also mainstream political support for those who wish to see the ban dropped. Most of this support is found in the Labour and Liberal Democratic Parties.

Defence spokesmen for the Labour Party have shown a commitment to ending the ban, as have the Liberal Democrats. However, it has never been a key part of their policy portfolios and, with the lessons of the Clinton Administration very fresh in British political minds, maybe it never will be.

Current Labour Party policy states: 'The Labour Party believes that homosexuality in itself is no reason for dismissal from the armed services. However, we do recognise that there are some difficulties. Other countries have addressed this issue and have ultimately been able to arrive at constructive solutions acceptable both to the Armed Forces and to society as a whole.'

It then states what will happen in the event of a Labour Party victory at the next election: 'A Labour Government will therefore establish a Commission to study the experiences of other nations and adopt the best practices toward evolving a solution in the British armed forces.'

If the commission is ever formed, perhaps it will look at the areas of British life where things have changed. When the American Federal General Accounting Office was asked by Congress to look into the issue of homosexuality in the armed forces it spoke to eight police and fire departments to see what was happening in this quasi-military environment. All but one had non-discrimination policies, some going back as far as the mid-1970s. None of the officials who were interviewed from these departments viewed homosexuality as a problem: they said that decisions to hire or fire were made on the basis of previous job performance, not on an individual's sexual orientation.

In fact, several of the departments' officials said that they felt the inclusion of homosexuals had had a positive impact on management-personnel relations.

The GAO report explained that the comparison with the police was thought relevant because of the elements of 'unit/ team cohesiveness', discipline and good order, morale, trust and confidence, and the system of command, rank and respect that are important to police and fire departments in achieving their 'overall mission'. The departments said that homosexuals and heterosexuals seemed to have acceptable working relationships, although they felt that this might be due to the sensitivity of the diversity and cultural awareness programmes that these departments had put in place.

In terms of security most of the officials whom the GAO spoke to said that, while many of the assignments carried out by the police were confidential or secret in nature, they felt that homosexuals whether 'closeted or admitted' were no more subject to breaches of security or blackmail than their heterosexual colleagues. Some of the officials stated that they felt exclusionary policies were counter-productive because they only created further stress.

In Britain a number of police forces now have equal opportunities policies that include clauses about sexuality.

Scott, a police constable in London, has recently 'come out' at work. His experiences over the last ten years show how attitudes and policies have changed in what a former Metropolitan Police Commissioner described as an increasingly military style of police force. Developments in the police might indicate how things could change in the armed forces.

Scott joined a small regional constabulary in 1984 and worked as a constable in a rural area. He had no contact with a gay community as there was no identifiable lesbian or gay group or venue in his area.

'We came across one or two individuals who were gay – but generally they were criminals and so didn't present a positive image. We were completely ignorant about gay people. I had a small-town childhood which was very religious and homosexuality was seen as ungodly and sinful. The subject was mentioned from time to time in a religious context, and it was seen as the result of an evil and ungodly life.

'For me the issue was particularly confusing, and I was aware of my homosexuality from a young age. I think I knew I was gay and accepted it in my mid to late teens, but I knew that this kind of behaviour would not be accepted in my close environment and so I concentrated on my studies and work and sports. I didn't have any wish to have a relationship with a woman and so didn't complicate things by having a relationship with anyone at all. I was eighteen when I joined the police, and I became increasingly aware of my need to be with my own sex, and that I wanted to form a relationship with someone of my own sex.'

Scott's paranoia about coming out, and the secretive nature of his first relationships, parallel quite closely the situation today in the armed forces.

'There was a married guy at another station who I was very friendly with. It was a male-bonding relationship that developed into a sexual one. But he wouldn't accept that he was gay. He wouldn't talk about it – he's still in that force, and it has taken him seven or eight years to come to terms with being gay.

'Colleagues talked about "shirtlifters" and would say that they should all be shot. Everyone was very ignorant – and it made it completely acceptable to say that gay people were not living a legitimate lifestyle. The general tone was that it was wrong. Canteen talk was very anti, but I can't say that I ever really stood up and said anything about it. Gay rights were a matter of ridicule then – Ken Livingstone was giving council flats to gays before families and we all said that was wrong. If I had said anything else it would have been seen as expressing very strange ideas. All my colleagues tended to be middle-class Tory types.'

In the police force of the 1980s it wasn't just the atmosphere that was similar to that in the armed forces. There was always the threat that if an officer was found to be gay he would be disciplined for 'conduct unbecoming a police officer'. Scott felt that he would receive no support from his superiors if he chose to come out.

'I was unhappy that there would be no opportunity in my force to stop living a lie and meet and begin having a relationship with another man. Whenever I met someone I had to be secretive about my job and I wanted to be myself. I applied to transfer to the Metropolitan Police in London. I was aware that there was a gay scene in London and that you could live that life as well – the place was big enough for you to be able to choose and live your own lifestyle separately from work. In the regions that just wasn't possible. It would be very difficult even now living a life as a gay man in the regional force I was in.

'So I came to London as a policeman in the late 1980s. I was immediately aware of the strong feelings in the police about the black and Asian communities as well as about the gay community, but over the following couple of years there was a definite change as management realised that these views had to change. In the older officers there were some deeply entrenched attitudes but there had to be a more open-minded approach to the ethnic communities. It was becoming unacceptable to be racist, but this did not extend to homosexuals. Whilst it became unacceptable to say "nigger" it was still completely OK to say "queer", "faggot" or "pervert".

'I was aware that in a large city you could have a complete break between work and play and there didn't have to be a conflict – although I was still conscious of the risk of being disciplined for "conduct unbecoming a police officer". I would have encountered many problems if I had come out at work. The AIDS panic and gay plague stories helped to keep most of my colleagues homophobic.'

The police force, like the services, is very disciplined with a rank and command structure. In many ways it is a similar 'club' to the armed forces, made up of people who are very conscious that they are not 'civilians'. It is a special status group within which homosexuality has never been an acceptable personal characteristic. Within the police force there is a strong need to fit in: you don't question authority or orders.

'The lower ranks do not feel that they have a right to question authority or claim their rights; everything is for Queen and country. For years the police believed that a person in a gay lifestyle was likely to be blackmailed – that you could be compromised because of the social stigma involved in being gay. But being gay is more acceptable now. Some time ago I couldn't have told my parents that I was gay, now I have.

'But I didn't reveal that I was gay at work for several years – not until I had told my family, whom I didn't want to find out from another source. I wanted them to accept me for who I was, a good police officer, responsible and professional. In ten years I have never taken my problems or relationship difficulties to work. Over the years I've been accepted and given glowing annual reports for my contact with the public, ability to detect crime, and understanding of the law. I have passed my promotion exams and have been a valuable member of the team. At the same time I have felt more confident about getting into relationships and able to talk about it with my family. The result of all the support from my family and friends has helped me to feel confident in talking to colleagues about what my position really is.

'My colleagues have been very supportive and have now met my partner and gay friends. A few years ago this would not have been possible. Then they were frightened of dealing with homosexuals, and now they go out and do the job with an "out" homosexual. People have asked me lots of questions and said, "You've changed my views completely," and, "You are a lot stronger than many straight people I know."

'Their stereotypes of gays are all wrong. For me working in a team we come up against violence a lot – and I sometimes think that as a gay man I deal with emotional situations better than many straight officers.

'In the last year I've attended a number of major public order incidents and been part of a police team in extremely violent situations. The fact that I am gay has not been relevant. I was at both Criminal Justice Bill demonstrations in 1994. I was in Whitehall when the crowd tried to storm Downing Street. We were subjected to an intense barrage of bottles, cans, sticks and other missiles. Thousands of people were screaming at us, "Kill the Bill, Kill the Bill." There were thousands of angry people, with absolute rage and hate on their faces and they wanted blood, they wanted to get us. The intimidation was enormous and we had to remain completely professional. If one of us had got caught on our own, then the crowd would have seriously assaulted or killed them. We had to work as a team and stay together. My colleagues know I'm gay and rely on me in these kind of situations.

'If my colleagues didn't really think I supported them properly then when I call for assistance if I'm under attack they could take a little longer to get to me. But when I'm on my own there has been no question that I'm one of the family – and we deal with a lot of violent situations. As a senior constable in central London most of my work revolves around crime arrests. I've worked in plain-clothes for long periods of time for and with CID, worked with surveillance teams, and liaised with drugs and firearm teams, and other agencies. I have shown myself to be competent in all these areas.

'On one occasion recently I was with a colleague when we went to a bookshop that was being burgled. I stopped one suspect outside and he caught two inside. They both went for him and started to attack him very violently. I could hear the noise and had to rush in to help him. I had a very violent struggle with a big guy who was hitting my colleague and I restrained him. He was headbutting and punching my colleague. If I hadn't been there he would have been very seriously injured indeed. My colleagues have good reason to trust me.

'If I encountered homophobia at work now with a colleague or someone else of junior rank, I would talk to them and give them the chance to retract or apologise. But if that didn't work, or the problem had come from someone senior I would have no hesitation in taking out the grievance procedures. We now have an equal opportunity policy and they would have to comply with that. They might have to attend an equal opportunities course and receive instruction on the issue, or if it had been really malicious they could face disciplinary procedures. The Metropolitan Police wants to attract ethnic minorities and lesbians and gays and therefore must be seen to be doing something about discrimination. I do believe now that the job would support me if I encountered any problems.

'I want to be a good police officer before I want to be a gay police officer . . . The fact that I am gay is incidental.'

There are major differences between the life of a police officer and a member of the armed forces – but the parallels are obvious too. As other areas of British life with similar military-style structures find that homosexuality is not incompatible with the successful fulfilment of their duties, the need for the Ministry of Defence to retain its ban looks less convincing. The Lesbian and Gay Police Association (LAGPA) is now formally recognised by the Metropolitan Police and consulted on various issues.

Like LAGPA, over recent years other lesbian and gay groups have grown in maturity, ability and reputation. By the 1992 General Election, the Tory Campaign for Homosexual Equality (TORCHE) and the Labour and Liberal-Democrat equivalents had become powerful minority voices in each of their political parties. The campaign to lower the age of sexual consent for gay men was, even if not a total victory in its achievement of a reduction from the age of twenty-one to eighteen, certainly a remarkable lobbying success. The campaign managed to combine groups as diverse as the British Medical Association, the children's charity Barnados and many leading churchmen in support of a lesbian and gay-run political campaign.

Some Members of Parliament said that they had never been aware of the numbers of lesbians and gay men in their constituencies before these men and women started writing to them about the age of consent.

In the 1980s homosexuals found a commercial voice in the power of their wallets: in the 1990s they seem to be discovering what they can do with the power of their votes, as they did in the United States some years earlier. The day when a gay voice in mainstream British politics is regularly heard has now arrived. It may not always achieve all that it hopes for, but it is certainly heard.

Across the political establishment lesbian and gay issues are on the agenda. John Major's Conservative Government removed the ban on lesbians and gay men serving in the civil service – and some of the officials I spoke to in the preparation of this book were gay. A Labour Government, if elected in 1996 or 1997, would probably set up a commission; although if Tony Blair watched the American experience in 1993 closely he will be wary of moving too quickly. In Mrs Thatcher's favourite television comedy, the accurately observed *Yes Minister*, civil servant Sir Humphrey Appleby's favourite device for creating interminable delay in the affairs of government was to set up an inquiry or commission. It will take continued lobbying by individuals and interested groups to ensure a positive change in policy, even with the supportive tone of the Labour Party's policy statement.

But this continued pressure is assured, as dismissed men and women are not now remaining silent. In the sober, conservative world in which most members of the armed forces live, homosexuality is only just beginning to be accepted as an alternative sexual identity. Those men and women who, like Robert Ely a few years ago would have contemplated killing themselves, are now declaring themselves publicly to be homosexual. Today they feel able to 'come out' and fight for their rights. They are contacting legal and support groups like Rank Outsiders, and approaching solicitors for advice. They are intending to sue.

Apart from the agenda for political change, the judicial route to change is also being tried. In September 1994 a group of lawyers and sacked servicemen and women met for the first time to discuss the way to challenge the Government's right to sack men and women solely on the grounds of their sexuality.

The armed forces are effectively excluded from most discrimination legislation, and the opportunities for legal redress for their members who believe that they have been unfairly treated are very limited. But the success of servicewomen, sacked for becoming pregnant, in the European Court, has led lawyers to believe that the Ministry of Defence is not as exempt from discrimination legislation as it had thought.

The court agreed with the women that, as members of the British armed forces have no opportunity for redress in the British courts over issues of sexual discrimination, they must have rights under the European Union's Equal Treatment Directive.

Jeanette Smithe, a nurse in the RAF was sacked on 25 November 1994 after five and a half years' service. The RAF withheld a substantial portion of her resettlement grant and refused to allow her to sit a very important professional exam two months after the investigation started. She is challenging the RAF's decision to sack her, and also the legality of withholding grants to which she believes she is entitled. Her solicitor, Madeleine Rees, was surprised by the RAF policy.

'They demand that some men and women continue to work after their investigation and yet in situations like Jeanette's when continuing at work would be of some appreciable benefit to the individual concerned, they send them home.'

Jeanette and her solicitor intend to challenged the RAF in the High Court – and believe they have a strong case. If the British court does not offer Jeanette the redress she is seeking, she hopes to carry on and challenge the Government in Europe.

RAF Sergeant Graeme Grady, who was dismissed on 16 December 1994, like every individual I spoke to when researching this book, was never told that he had a right to appeal against his discharge. Acting under legal advice, he tried to have his dismissal delayed while he made a formal complaint about the final decision to sack him.

In the event his request to remain in the RAF while he challenged his dismissal was denied by the Ministry of Defence, Graeme hopes to apply to the courts for an injunction to prevent the RAF from dismissing him, pending the completion of their own internal procedures.

Royal Navy Lieutenant-Commander Duncan Lustig-Prean, who is still waiting to be told what will happen to him seven months after he 'came out', has prepared the ground carefully for the weeks after he receives the letter he anticipates telling him that he too is being sacked. He will appeal against the decision to the Admiralty Board, to the Queen, to the High Court and to Europe. Duncan says that he is not going to be sacked without a fight.

Peter Duffy, a prominent 'Euro-lawyer', believes that with a variety of different routes open to sacked servicemen and women, they have a strong chance of success. With men and women intending to challenge the ban through the courts in every way that they can, and with an increasing level of political support for the removal of the policy, I would be surprised if the ban lasts in its current form until the turn of the century.

Lesbians and gay men are determined to win the right, by judicial or political means, to serve openly in the British armed forces – alongside the many thousands of homosexuals who already do, in secret. The Ministry of Defence still views the groups and individuals who are fighting for this right as anti-establishment: perhaps in a different time and place their desire would have been described as patriotism. Watch this space.